Rick Steves®

POCKE

ATH

Rick Steves with Gene Openshaw
and Cameron Hewitt

Contents

Post-Pandemic Travels: Expect a Warm Welcome...and a Few Changes
Research for this guidebook was limited by the COVID-19 outbreak, and the long-term impact of the crisis on our recommended destinations is unclear. Some details in this book will change for post-pandemic travelers. Now more than ever, it's smart to reconfirm specifics as you plan and travel. As always, you can find major updates at RickSteves.com/update.

Introduction

Traveling to Athens is like making a pilgrimage to the cradle of our civilization. Romantics can't help but get goose bumps as they kick around the same pebbles that once stuck in Socrates' sandals, with the floodlit Parthenon forever floating ethereally overhead. You'll walk in the footsteps of the great minds that created democracy, philosophy, theater, and more...even when you're dodging motorcycles on "pedestrianized" streets.

While sprawling and congested, the city has a compact, user-friendly tourist zone, with sights such as the Acropolis Museum and the Ancient Agora an easy walk apart. Many locals speak English, major landmarks are well-signed, and most street signs are in both Greek and English.

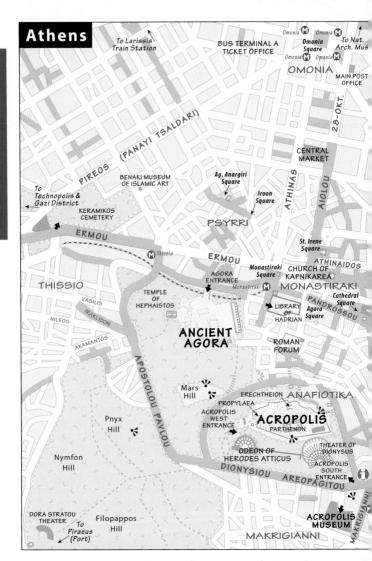

INTRODUCTION

Athens

To Larissis Train Station

BUS TERMINAL A TICKET OFFICE

Omonia Ⓜ Omonia Ⓜ

To Nat. Arch. Mus

Omonia Square

Omonia Ⓜ Omonia Ⓜ

OMONIA

MAIN POST OFFICE

PIREOS (PANAYI TSALDARI)

BENAKI MUSEUM OF ISLAMIC ART

Ag. Anargiri Square

Iroon Square

28-OKT.

CENTRAL MARKET

ATHINAS

AIOLOU

To Technopolis & Gazi District

KERAMIKOS CEMETERY

PSYRRI

ERMOU

Ⓜ Thissio

ERMOU

St. Irene Square

THISSIO

AGORA ENTRANCE

Monastiraki Square

ATHINAIDOS

CHURCH OF KAPNIKAREA

VASILIS

TEMPLE OF HEPHAISTOS

Monastiraki Ⓜ

MONASTIRAKI

NILEOS

Cathedral Square

PANDROSSOU

LIBRARY OF HADRIAN

Agora Square

IRAKLIDON

AKAMANTOS

ANCIENT AGORA

ROMAN FORUM

APOSTOLOU PAVLOU

Mars Hill

ERECHTHEION

ANAFIOTIKA

PROPYLAEA

ACROPOLIS WEST ENTRANCE

ACROPOLIS

PARTHENON

Pnyx Hill

Nymfon Hill

ODEON OF HERODES ATTICUS

THEATER OF DIONYSUS

ACROPOLIS SOUTH ENTRANCE

DIONYSIOU AREOPAGITOU

Ⓘ

MAKRIGIANNI

DORA STRATOU THEATER

To Piraeus (Port)

Filopappos Hill

ACROPOLIS MUSEUM

MAKRIGIANNI

EXARCHIA

CHAR. TRIKOUPI
SOLONOS
AKADIMIAS
PANEPISTIMIOU

NATIONAL
LIBRARY

THEATRICAL
MUSEUM

ATHENS
UNIVERSITY

Panepistimio Ⓜ

ELEFTHERIOU VENIZELOU

KORAI

*Klafthmonos
Square*

MUSEUM
OF THE CITY
OF ATHENS

STADIOU

KOLOKOTRONI

SYNTAGMA

PERIKLEOUS

ERMOU

CATHEDRAL
(MITROPOLIS)

KOLOKOTRONI

Bus #180
to / from
Piraeus

Ⓑ

*Syntagma
Square*

Ⓜ
Syntagma

Bus #X95
to Airport Ⓑ

PARLIAMENT

BENAKI MUSEUM
OF GREEK HISTORY
& CULTURE

VASILISSIS

MUSEUM
OF CYCLADIC
ART

SOFIAS

To Ⓜ
Evangel-
ismos

NATIONAL
WAR MUS.

BYZANTINE
& CHRISTIAN
MUSEUM

To
Airport

KOLONAKI

Lykavittos Hill

To
Lykavittos
Theater

FUNICULAR

300 Meters
300 Yards

PLAKA

ADRIANOU

VASILISSIS AMALIAS

*Filomousou
Square*

ARCH OF
HADRIAN

Ⓑ
Bus #X80
from Piraeus

Ⓑ
Bus #X80
to Piraeus

← *Akropoli*

TEMPLE OF
OLYMPIAN
ZEUS

ATHANASIOU
DIAKOU

VASILISSIS OLGAS

ARDITTOU

NATIONAL
GARDEN

ZAPPEION

VASILEOS KONSTANTINOU

PANGRATI

*Stadium
Square*

PANATHENAIC
STADIUM

INTRODUCTION

About This Book

Rick Steves Pocket Athens is a personal tour guide...in your pocket. The core of the book is five self-guided walks and tours that zero in on Athens' greatest sights and experiences. My Athens City Walk leads you on a three-part stroll through the engaging and refreshingly small city center. My Ancient Agora and Acropolis tours take you back in time to the bustling religious and commercial centers of ancient Greece. And the Acropolis Museum and National Archaeological Museum provide up-close views of artifacts and treasures unearthed from Greece's great ancient sites.

The rest of this book is a traveler's tool kit, with my best advice on how to save money, plan your time, use public transportation, and avoid lines at the busiest sights. You'll also get recommendations on hotels, restaurants, and activities.

Athens by Neighborhood

Most of Athens is a noisy, polluted modern sprawl: characterless, poorly planned, and hastily erected concrete suburbs that house the area's rapidly expanding population. But most visitors barely see that part of Athens. Almost everything of importance to tourists is within a few blocks of the Acropolis.

A good map is a necessity for enjoying Athens on foot. The fine map the TI gives out works great. You'll concentrate on the following districts:

The Plaka (PLAH-kah, Πλάκα): This neighborhood at the foot of the Acropolis is the core of the tourist's Athens. One of the only parts of town that's atmospheric and Old World-feeling, it's also the most crassly touristic (souvenir shops and tourist-oriented tavernas).

Monastiraki (moh-nah-stee-RAH-kee, Μοναστηρακι): This area ("Little Monastery") borders the Plaka to the northwest, surrounding the square of the same name. It's known for its handy Metro stop (where line 1/green meets line 3/blue), seedy flea market, and souvlaki stands.

Psyrri (psee-REE, Ψυρρή): Formerly a dumpy ghetto just north of Monastiraki, Psyrri is now a thriving dining and nightlife district—one of central Athens' most appealing areas to explore.

Syntagma (SEEN-dag-mah, Σύνταγμα): Centered on Athens' main square, Syntagma ("Constitution") Square, this urban-feeling

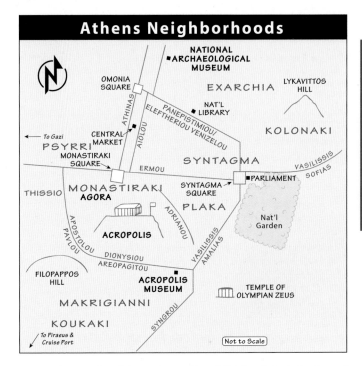

Athens Neighborhoods

NATIONAL ARCHAEOLOGICAL MUSEUM

OMONIA SQUARE

EXARCHIA

LYKAVITTOS HILL

NAT'L LIBRARY

PANEPISTIMIOU/ ELEFTHERIOU VENIZELOU

ATHINAS

AIOLOU

KOLONAKI

← To Gazi

CENTRAL MARKET

PSYRRI

MONASTIRAKI SQUARE

ERMOU

SYNTAGMA

VASILISSIS SOFIAS

THISSIO

MONASTIRAKI

AGORA

SYNTAGMA SQUARE

PARLIAMENT

PLAKA

ADRIANOU

Nat'l Garden

ACROPOLIS

APOSTOLOU PAVLOU

DIONYSIOU AREOPAGITOU

VASILISSIS AMALIAS

FILOPAPPOS HILL

ACROPOLIS MUSEUM

TEMPLE OF OLYMPIAN ZEUS

MAKRIGIANNI

KOUKAKI

SYNGROU

↙ To Piraeus & Cruise Port

Not to Scale

zone melts into the Plaka to the south. While the Plaka is dominated by tourist shops, Syntagma is where local urbanites do their shopping.

Thissio (thee-SEE-oh, Θησείο): West of the Ancient Agora, Thissio is an upscale, local-feeling residential neighborhood with lots of outdoor cafés and restaurants. It's easily accessible thanks to the handy "Acropolis Loop" pedestrian walkway bordering the base of the Acropolis.

Gazi (GAH-zee, Γκάζι): At the western edge of the tourist's Athens (just beyond Thissio and Psyrri), Gazi is trendy and artsy, with lots of nightclubs and younger-skewing eateries. Its centerpiece is a former gas-works-turned-events center called Technopolis.

Makrigianni (mah-kree-YAH-nee, Μακρυγιάννη) and **Koukaki** (koo-KAH-kee, Κουκάκι): Tucked just behind (south of) the Acropolis,

Athens at a Glance

▲▲▲**Acropolis** The most important ancient site in the Western world, where Athenians built their architectural masterpiece, the Parthenon. **Hours:** Daily 8:00-20:00, Oct until 18:00, Nov-March until 17:00. See page 65.

▲▲▲**Acropolis Museum** Modern temple for ancient art. **Hours:** Daily 8:00-20:00 except Mon until 16:00, Fri until 22:00; Nov-March Mon-Thu 9:00-17:00, Fri until 22:00, Sat-Sun until 20:00. See page 93.

▲▲▲**Ancient Agora** Social and commercial center of ancient Athens, with a well-preserved temple and an intimate museum. **Hours:** Daily 8:00-20:00, Oct until 18:00, Nov-March until 15:00. See page 45.

▲▲▲**National Archaeological Museum** World's best collection of ancient Greek art. **Hours:** Daily 8:00-20:00 except Tue from 12:30; Nov-March 9:00-16:00 (Tue from 12:30). See page 109.

▲▲**"Acropolis Loop"** Traffic-free pedestrian walkways ringing much of the Acropolis with vendors, cafés, and special events. See page 134.

▲▲**Temple of Olympian Zeus** Remains of the largest temple in ancient Greece. **Hours:** Daily 8:00-20:00, Oct until 18:00, Nov-March until 15:00. See page 136.

▲▲**Psyrri** Vibrant neighborhood near the center, great for eating, exploring, and escaping other tourists. See page 142.

these overlapping urban neighborhoods within easy walking distance of the ancient sites make a good home base if you want to escape the crowds.

Kolonaki (koh-loh-NAH-kee, Κολωνάκι): Just north and east of the Parliament/Syntagma Square area, this upscale diplomatic quarter, with several good museums and a yuppie dining zone, huddles under the tall, pointy Lykavittos Hill.

Major Streets: The base of the Acropolis is partially encircled by a broad traffic-free walkway, named **Dionysiou Areopagitou** (Διονυσίου Αρεοπαγίτου) to the south and **Apostolou Pavlou** (Αποστόλου Παύλου) to the west; for simplicity, I call these the **"Acropolis Loop."** Touristy **Adrianou** street (Αδριανού) curves through the Plaka a few blocks away from the Acropolis' base. Partly

▲▲**Benaki Museum of Greek History and Culture** Exquisite collection of artifacts from the ancient, Byzantine, Ottoman, and modern eras. **Hours:** Wed-Mon 10:00-18:00 except Thu until 24:00, Sun until 16:00, closed Tue. See page 143.

▲▲**Museum of Cycladic Art** World's largest compilation of Cycladic art, from 4,000 years ago. **Hours:** Wed-Mon 10:00-17:00 except Thu until 20:00, Sun from 11:00, closed Tue. See page 144.

▲▲**Byzantine and Christian Museum** Fascinating look at the Byzantines, who put their own stamp on Greek and Roman culture. **Hours:** Daily 8:00-20:00 except Tue from 12:30. See page 145.

▲**Mars Hill** Historic spot—with a classic view of the Acropolis—where the Apostle Paul preached to the Athenians. See page 135.

▲**Syntagma Square** Famous public space with a popular changing-of-the-guard ceremony five minutes before the top of each hour. See page 140.

▲**Panathenaic (a.k.a. "Olympic") Stadium** Gleaming marble stadium restored to its second-century AD condition. **Hours:** Daily 8:00-19:00, Nov-Feb until 17:00. See page 142.

Sights generally keep consistent morning opening hours but can close earlier than listed. Many closing times depend on the sunset. Check locally.

pedestrianized **Ermou** street (Ερμού) runs west from Syntagma Square, defining the Plaka, Monastiraki, and Thissio to the south and Psyrri to the north. Where Ermou meets Monastiraki, **Athinas** street (Αθηνάς) heads north to Omonia Square.

Planning Your Time

The following day-plans give an idea of how much an organized, motivated, and caffeinated person can see. Athens' top sights—the Acropolis, Ancient Agora, Acropolis Museum, and National Archaeological Museum—deserve about two hours apiece. Two days total is plenty of time for the casual tourist to see the city's main attractions and have a little time left over for exploring (or to add more museums).

Day 1: In the morning, follow my Athens City Walk, then grab a souvlaki at Monastiraki. After lunch, as the crowds subside, visit the ancient biggies: First tour the Ancient Agora, then hike up to the Acropolis (confirm how late it's open). Be the last person off the Acropolis. Stroll down the Dionysiou Areopagitou pedestrian boulevard, then promenade to dinner—in Thissio, Monastiraki, Psyrri, or the Plaka.

Day 2: Spend the morning visiting the Acropolis Museum and exploring the Plaka. After lunch, head to the National Archaeological Museum.

Day 3 and Beyond: Head out toward Kolonaki to take in some of Athens' "also-ran" museums—the Benaki Museum of Greek History and Culture, Museum of Cycladic Art, and Byzantine and Christian Museum. Or consider ditching Athens for a long but satisfying day trip to Delphi, a sweet getaway to the isle of Hydra, or a quick dip into the Peloponnese peninsula, with the charming port town of Nafplio and the famous ancient sites of Epidavros and Mycenae. Even better, spend the night.

When to Go

Tourist season is roughly Easter through October. Peak season is summer, when Athens is packed with tourists, and hotel prices can be high. July and August are the hottest. The best time to visit is late spring (May) and fall (Sept-Oct). It's pleasant, with comfortable weather, no rain, and smaller crowds (except during holiday weekends).

Winter (late Oct through mid-March) is colder, with some rainfall. Sights may close during lunch, TI offices keep shorter hours, and

Rick's Free Video Clips and Audio Tours

Rick Steves Classroom Europe, a powerful tool for teachers, is also useful for travelers. This video library contains over 400 short clips excerpted from my public television series. Enjoy these videos as you sort through options for your trip and to better understand what you'll see in Europe. Check it out at Classroom.RickSteves.com (just enter a topic to find everything I've filmed on a subject).

    Rick Steves Audio Europe, a free app, makes it easy to download my audio tours and listen to them offline as you travel. For this book (look for the 🎧), these audio tours include my Athens City Walk and tours of the Acropolis, Ancient Agora, and National Archaeological Museum. The app also offers interviews from my public radio show with experts from Europe and around the globe. Find it in your app store or at RickSteves.com/AudioEurope.

some tourist activities vanish altogether. Hotel rates are soft; look for bargains.

Before You Go

You'll have a smoother trip if you tackle a few things ahead of time. For more info on these topics, see the Practicalities chapter (and RickSteves.com, which has helpful travel tips and talks).

    Make sure your travel documents are valid. If your passport is due to expire within six months of your ticketed date of return, you need to renew it. Allow up to six weeks to renew or get a passport (www.travel.state.gov). You may also need to register with the European Travel Information and Authorization System (ETIAS).

    Arrange your transportation. Book your international flights. Figure out your transportation options. If traveling beyond Athens, it's worth thinking about renting a car, buying boat tickets, or booking flights to the islands. (You can wing it once you're there, but tickets may cost more or be sold out.) Drivers: Consider bringing an International Driving Permit (sold at AAA offices in the US, www.aaa.com) along with your license.

    Book rooms well in advance, especially if your trip falls during peak season or any major holidays or festivals.

Consider travel insurance. Compare the cost of the insurance to the cost of your potential loss. Check whether your existing insurance (health, homeowners, or renters) covers you and your possessions overseas.

Call your bank. Alert your bank that you'll be using your debit and credit cards in Europe. Ask about transaction fees, and get the PIN number for your credit card. You don't need to bring along euros; you can withdraw euros from cash machines in Europe.

Use your smartphone smartly. Sign up for an international service plan to reduce your costs, or rely on Wi-Fi in Europe instead. Download any apps you'll want on the road, such as maps, translators, transit schedules, and Rick Steves Audio Europe (see sidebar).

Pack light. You'll walk with your luggage more than you think. I travel for weeks with a single carry-on bag and a daypack. Use the packing checklist in Practicalities as a guide.

Travel Smart

If you have a positive attitude, equip yourself with good information (this book), and expect to travel smart, you will.

Pickpockets abound in crowded places where tourists congregate. Treat commotions as smokescreens for theft. Keep your cash,

credit cards, and passport secure in a money belt tucked under your clothes; carry only a day's spending money in your front pocket or wallet.

If you wilt easily, choose a hotel with air-conditioning, start your day early, take a midday siesta at your hotel, and resume your sightseeing later.

Be sure to schedule in slack time for picnics, laundry, people-watching, leisurely dinners, shopping, and recharging your touristic batteries. Slow down and be open to unexpected experiences and the hospitality of the Greek people.

Sip a frappé while relaxing at a café, order souvlaki from a hole in the wall, or try ouzo at a bar for locals. As you visit places I know and love, I'm happy you'll be meeting some of my favorite Greeks.

Happy travels! *Kalo taxidi!*

Athens City Walk

This walk takes you through the striking contrasts of the city center—
from chaotic, traffic-clogged urban zones, to sleepy streets packed
with bearded priests shopping for a new robe or chalice, to peaceful,
barely-wide-enough-for-a-donkey back lanes that twist their way up
toward the Acropolis. The walk begins at Syntagma Square, mean-
ders through the fascinating old Plaka district, and finishes at lively
Monastiraki Square (near the Ancient Agora, markets, good restaurants, and a handy Metro stop). This sightseeing spine will help you get
a once-over-lightly look at Athens, which you can use as a springboard
for diving into the city's various colorful sights and neighborhoods.

ORIENTATION

Length of This Walk: Allow plenty of time. This three-part walk takes two hours without stops or detours. But if you explore and dip into sights here and there—pausing to ponder a dimly lit Orthodox church or doing some window (or actual) shopping—it can enjoyably eat up a half-day or more. This walk is also easy to break up—stop after Part 2 and return for Part 3 later.

When to Go: Do this walk early in your visit, as it can help you get your bearings in this potentially confusing city. Morning is best, since many churches close for an afternoon break, and other sights—including the Acropolis—are too crowded to enjoy by midmorning.

Getting There: The walk begins at Syntagma Square, just northeast of the Plaka tourist zone. It's a short walk from the recommended Plaka hotels; if you're staying away from the city center, get here by Metro (stop: Syntagma).

Churches: Athens' churches are free but keep irregular hours—generally daily 8:30-13:30 and some evenings (17:00-19:30). If you want to buy candles at churches (as the locals do), be sure to have a few small coins.

Cathedral: Free, likely open daily 8:00-19:00 (closed 13:00-16:30 off-season).

Temple of Olympian Zeus: €6, covered by Acropolis combo-ticket (for details, see sidebar on page 135); daily 8:00-20:00, Oct until 18:00, Nov-March until 15:00.

Roman Forum: €6, covered by Acropolis combo-ticket, daily 8:00-20:00, shorter hours off-season.

Library of Hadrian: €4, covered by Acropolis combo-ticket, daily 8:00-20:00, shorter hours off-season.

Tours: ∩ Download my free Athens City Walk audio tour.

Dress Code: Modest dress in churches—no bare shoulders or shorts—is encouraged.

Starring: Athens' top squares, churches, and Roman ruins, connected by bustling urban streets that are alternately choked with cars and mopeds, or thronged by pedestrians, vendors...and fellow tourists.

This lengthy walk has three parts: The first introduces modern Athens, centered on Syntagma Square and the Ermou shopping street. The second part focuses on Athens' Greek Orthodox faith, with visits to three interesting churches. And the third part is a wander through the old core of Athens, including the charming-but-touristy Plaka, the mellow Greek-village-on-a-hillside of Anafiotika, and some impressive ancient monuments. In a sense, we'll be walking back in time—from bustling modern Athens, through its mystical medieval period, to the place where the city was born: the Acropolis.

Part 1: Modern Athens

This first part of the walk lets you feel the pulse of a modern capital.

▶ *Start at Syntagma Square. From the leafy park at the center of the square, climb to the top of the stairs and stand across the street from the big Greek Parliament building.*

❶ Syntagma Square (Plateia Syntagmatos)

Here in Syntagma Square (SEEN-dag-mah) you're in the heart of this great capital, and in many ways the heart of the entire Greek nation. Here is where the nation is governed. It's where citizens gather for angry demonstrations and national celebrations—the "Times Square" of Greece. Surrounding the square are posh hotels, major banks, and the Greek Parliament. Beneath your feet is the city's busiest Metro stop. Around the edges, the streets are choked with buses, cars, taxis, and mopeds. And in the fountain-dotted square, Athenians go about their business: hustling off to work, handing out leaflets, feeding pigeons, listening to street musicians, or just enjoying a park bench in the shade.

From here, sightseeing options spin off through the city like spokes on a wheel. Face the Parliament building (east), and get oriented. To the left is the head of Vasilissis Sofias avenue, lined with embassies and museums, including the Benaki Museum of Greek History and Culture, Museum of Cycladic Art, Byzantine and Christian Museum, and National War Museum. This boulevard leads to the ritzy Kolonaki quarter, with its high-end shopping promenades and funicular up to the top of Lykavittos Hill.

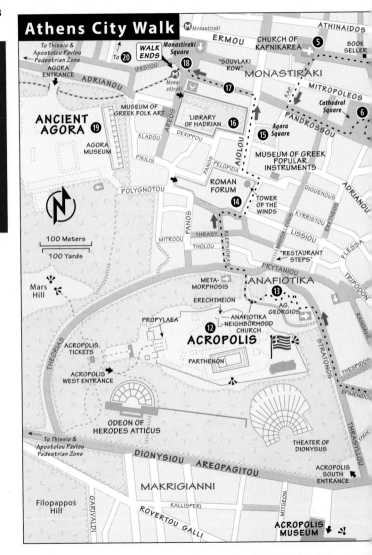

Athens City Walk

Ⓜ Monastiraki

ATHINAIDOS

ERMOU CHURCH OF KAPNIKAREA ⑤ BOOK SELLER

To Thissio & Apostolou Pavlou Pedestrian Zone

To ⑳

WALK ENDS

Monastiraki Square

Ⓜ ⑱

"SOUVLAKI ROW" MONASTIRAKI

IFESTOU

AGORA ENTRANCE

ADRIANOU

Mona-straki Ⓜ

⑰

KAP MITROPOLEOS

Cathedral Square ⑥

MUSEUM OF GREEK FOLK ART

AREOS

LIBRARY OF HADRIAN ⑯

PANDROSSOU

ANCIENT AGORA ⑲

KLADOU DEXIPPOU

Agora Square ⑮

AGORA MUSEUM

PIKILIS

PANOS PELOPIDA

AIOLOU

MUSEUM OF GREEK POPULAR INSTRUMENTS

ADRIANOU

POLYGNOTOU

ROMAN FORUM ⑭

DIOGENOUS

TOWER OF THE WINDS

KYRRISTOU

ERETHEOS

PANOS

MITROOU THRASY THOLOU

KLEPSIDRAS

MNISIKLEOUS LISSIOU

FLESSA

"RESTAURANT STEPS"

PRYTANIOU

TRIPODON

100 Meters

100 Yards

Mars Hill

META-MORPHOSIS

ANAFIOTIKA ⑬

ERECHTHEION

AG. GEORGIOS

RANGAVA

PROPYLAEA

ANAFIOTIKA NEIGHBORHOOD CHURCH

ACROPOLIS TICKETS

⑫ ACROPOLIS

STRATONOS

THEORIAS

ACROPOLIS WEST ENTRANCE

PARTHENON

THESPIDOS

EPIMENIDO

ODEON OF HERODES ATTICUS

THEATER OF DIONYSUS

THRASYLLOU

To Thissio & Apostolou Pavlou Pedestrian Zone

ACROPOLIS SOUTH ENTRANCE

DIONYSIOU AREOPAGITOU

Filopappos Hill

MAKRIGIANNI

KALLISPERI

MITSEON

ACROPOLIS MUSEUM

GARIVALDI

ROVERTOU GALLI

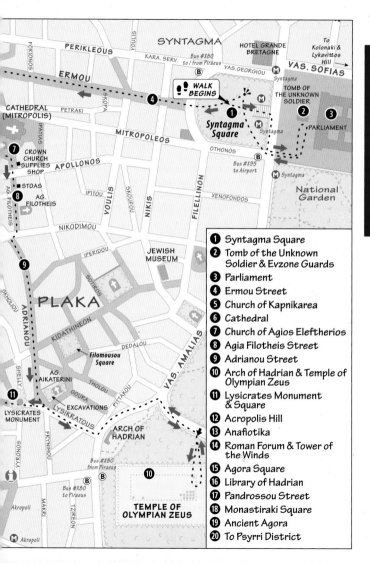

1 Syntagma Square
2 Tomb of the Unknown Soldier & Evzone Guards
3 Parliament
4 Ermou Street
5 Church of Kapnikarea
6 Cathedral
7 Church of Agios Eleftherios
8 Agia Filotheis Street
9 Adrianou Street
10 Arch of Hadrian & Temple of Olympian Zeus
11 Lysicrates Monument & Square
12 Acropolis Hill
13 Anafiotika
14 Roman Forum & Tower of the Winds
15 Agora Square
16 Library of Hadrian
17 Pandrossou Street
18 Monastiraki Square
19 Ancient Agora
20 To Psyrri District

Syntagma Square—center of modern Athens   National Garden—Athens' Central Park

Extending behind and to the right of the Parliament building is the National Garden, Athens' "Central Park." Here you'll find the Zappeion mansion-turned-conference-hall (with a fine summer outdoor cinema nearby) and, beyond the greenery, the evocative, ancient Panathenaic Stadium.

This area is also one of Athens' prime transit hubs, with many bus stops and the city's busiest Metro station.

Behind you, at the west end of the square, stretches the traffic-free shopping street called Ermou, which heads to the Plaka neighborhood and Monastiraki Square. (We'll be heading that way soon.)

Syntagma Square is a breezy oasis, shaded with a variety of trees: cypress, plane, palm, orange, and laurel. Breathe deeply and ponder the fact that until 1990, Athens was the most polluted city in Europe.

But over the last two decades, Athens has worked hard to clean up its act. Traffic is now restricted in the city center. Check out the license plates of passenger cars. Only cars with even-numbered license plates are allowed in on certain days of the week—those with odd numbers are allowed on the other days. The rich get around it by owning two cars. The city has instituted other green policies—more pedestrian zones, better public transit, and cleaner heating fuel. Thanks to this, 21st-century Athens is a much more livable place.

While the Acropolis and the Agora were the heart of ancient Athens, Syntagma has been the city center for the last two centuries. Whenever the Greek people have needed to speak their mind, they've gathered here to do it. For that part of Athens' story, turn your attention to our next stop—the Parliament.

▶ *Using the crosswalk (one on either side of Syntagma Square), cross the busy street. Directly in front of the Parliament you'll see the...*

❷ Tomb of the Unknown Soldier and the Evzone Guards

In the nation that invented democracy, nothing epitomizes its modern struggle for self-rule so much as this spot.

Here you'll find Greece's Tomb of the Unknown Soldier, guarded by the fancifully dressed evzone guards. The tomb itself is simple—a marble slab marked only with a cross. Carved into the wall above is an image of a fallen warrior from ancient times, with helmet and shield. On either side are the names of great battles in Greek history since 1821.

The much-photographed evzone, clad in traditional pleated kilts, white britches, and shoes with pom-poms, are soldiers from an elite infantry unit of the Greek army. The soldiers do a ceremonial changing of the guard at five minutes before the top of each hour. There's also a less elaborate crossing on the half-hour. During the ceremonies, they march with a slow-motion, high-stepping gait to their new positions. Once there, they stand ramrod straight, just begging for some clown to pose at their side. A full changing-of-the-guard ceremony, complete with marching band, takes place most Sundays at 11:00.

The guards remind Greeks of the crucial moment when modern Greece was born. The year was 1821. After nearly four centuries under the thumb of the Ottoman Turks, the Greeks rose up. They were led by ragtag bands of mountain guerrilla fighters. Their uniforms were modeled after ancient warriors, complete with Mycenaean pom-poms. Today's evzone guards proudly wear the same outfit. In fact, their winter skirts have exactly 400 pleats...one for each year of Ottoman occupation (and don't you forget it).

The Greek War of Independence became a kind of cause célèbre throughout Europe. Even the English poet Lord Byron donned

Evzone guards at the tomb

Their colorful outfits draw a crowd.

a uniform like this and gave his life for the cause of Greek freedom. Finally, in 1829, the rebels drove the Ottomans out. However, no sooner had they driven out the Ottomans, when they got...an Otto.

▶ *For the rest of the story, take a step back for a view of the...*

❸ Parliament

Although this grand building now houses Greek democracy, it began life as a palace for a despotic king. After Greece gained its independence, the first government was so weak (with a capital in far-off Nafplio) that Europe's powers-that-be installed an outsider to rule as king.

In 1832, Prince Otto of Bavaria, just 17 years old, became King Otto of Greece. He moved the capital to Athens and built himself a magnificent royal palace—today's Parliament building.

However, the Greeks, having just freed themselves from Ottoman rule, chafed under this dictatorial Bavarian monarch. On September 3, 1843, angry rioters gathered in the square to protest. Wisely, King Otto stepped onto the balcony of this building, quieted the mob, and gave them exactly what they wanted—a democratic constitution. Modern Athens was born, and the square was dubbed "Syntagma"—the Greek word for constitution.

It was King Otto who shaped the look of modern Athens. His architects (imported from Bavaria) created a grand European capital in the Neoclassical style. Broad new boulevards were blasted through, punctuated with vast squares like Syntagma. Otto revived elements from the classical world—things like the Greek columns and triangular pediments you see on the Parliament building.

This set the tone for buildings like the opulent **Hotel Grande**

Parliament overlooking Syntagma Square

Neoclassical Hotel Grande Bretagne

The Story of Athens

Athens emerged as a major city around 500 BC. But when Persia invaded (480 BC), Athens was burned to the ground. The Athenians rallied, united their fellow Greeks, drove the Persians out...and the Greek Golden Age began.

From 450 to 400 BC, Athens reigned supreme. Its population was about 100,000. The Acropolis and the Agora marked the center of town. Athens' high culture set the tone for Western civilization. By the time of the conqueror Alexander the Great (c. 333 BC), Greek culture had spread throughout the known world, with Athens as the capital of this vast "Hellenistic" empire.

When the Romans arrived (146 BC), they made Athens their regional capital, erecting even greater temples, theaters, and forums. But as the Roman Empire declined, so did Athens. A horrendous barbarian invasion in the third century BC left the city in ashes. When Rome fell in 476 AD, Greece came under the sway of the Byzantine Empire—that is, the eastern half of the empire that didn't fall. For the next thousand years, Athens was ruled from far-off Constantinople (modern Istanbul). Now Eastern Orthodox, Athens was soon dotted with impressive Orthodox churches filled with glorious mosaics.

In 1453, Constantinople fell to the Ottoman Turks, and Athens came under the rule of Muslim sultans. The Parthenon became a mosque, the city became a rural backwater, and its population shrank to just 2,000.

In 1821, Athens' rebirth began. The Greeks rose up, evicted the Ottomans, and demanded self-rule. They rebuilt Athens in the Neoclassical style, with broad boulevards and a new city center at Syntagma Square. The city grew even more after World War I, when thousands of refugees poured in, and after World War II, when starving Greek peasants from the countryside flooded Athens looking for work. In the last half of the 20th century, Athens' population exploded from one million to nearly four million.

For years, there was lots of ugly urban sprawl and cheap housing. But the 2004 Olympic Games brought major improvements in infrastructure, public transportation, green policies, and an overall beautification program. Today, the city is a major European cultural capital and attractive tourist destination.

Bretagne (to the right as you face Syntagma Square). All over town, you'll see pastel-colored buildings highlighted in white trim. The rectangular windows, flanked by white Greek half-columns, are fronted by balconies and topped with cornices. Many of the buildings themselves are also framed at the top with cornices. As you continue on this walk, you'll see a few surviving Neoclassical buildings, as well as modern buildings mimicking their geometric symmetry.

Today, the Parliament building is where 300 elected representatives tend to the business of state for the Greek nation. (Or, as more cynical locals would say, tend to the business of setting themselves up for cushy, post-political lives.)

▸ *One of the grandest of Otto's new streets was the one that spilled directly out the bottom of Syntagma Square. And that's where we're headed next—Ermou Street.*

To get there, cross back to Syntagma Square and head to the bottom of the square. Near the McDonald's you'll find the start of the traffic-free boulevard called...

❹ Ermou Street

This pedestrian mall called Ermou (air-MOO) is the modern city's main axis. As you stroll, you'll see a mix of modern and traditional, global and local.

There are lots of international clothing chain stores, some of them housed in elegant Neoclassical mansions with ironwork balconies. All of Athens walks along here: businessmen buying a daily paper, teenage girls cruising the mall, hawkers selling lottery tickets, Orthodox priests stroking their beards. You'll see old men twirling worry beads and young activists gathering signatures.

Keep an eye out for people selling local snacks—including pretzel-like sesame rings (called *koulouri*) and slices of fresh coconut. At #13 (two blocks down on the left) is Gregory's, the popular "Greek Starbucks" coffee chain with its distinctive green logo.

While Ermou street has long been the place to shop for women's clothing, many traditional boutiques have been replaced by chain stores. These appeal to young Athenians, but older folks prefer the hole-in-the-wall boutiques to the right (on streets like Perikleous, Lekka, and Kolokotroni).

As you continue down Ermou street, think of how much Athens has changed in the last two centuries. In 1800, this neighborhood was a run-down village of dirt alleyways. Then streets like Ermou were blasted through as part of the city's revival. But the turbulent 20th-century turned the once-chic street into all that was once so terrible about Athens: ugly modern buildings, tacky neon signs, double-parked trucks, and noisy traffic. When Ermou was first pedestrianized in 2000, merchants were upset. Now they love the ambience of this people-friendly shopping zone.

After passing Evaggelistrias street, look for the little **book wagon** carrying on a long tradition. They sell colorful, old-fashioned books, including alphabet books (labeled αλφαβητaριο, *alphabetario*), which have been reprinted for nostalgic older Greeks. The English word "alphabet" comes from the first two Greek letters (alpha, beta).

▶ *Ermou street leads straight to our next stop—a little brick church stranded in the middle of the road amid all this commercial bustle. You can't miss it.*

Part 2: The Greek Orthodox Church

In the fourth century AD, the Roman Empire split in half, dividing Europe down the middle. Over the centuries, Western Christians gravitated toward the pope in Rome as their spiritual head, while Easterners turned to the patriarch in Constantinople (Istanbul), each developing slightly different beliefs and ways of worship. In 1054, the Great Schism between the pope and the patriarch made that division between Roman Catholicism and Eastern Orthodox official, and the Orthodox Church split into about a dozen regional branches—Greek Orthodox, Russian Orthodox, Serbian Orthodox, and so on. The Greek constitution recognizes Orthodox Christianity as the "prevailing" religion of Greece. The archbishop of Athens is Greece's "pope."

This part of our walk introduces you to the Orthodox faith of Greece, including stops at three different churches. The first of our churches is one of Athens' oldest—from medieval times, when Greece was part of the Byzantine Empire (AD 323-1453).

❺ Church of Kapnikarea

Built around the year 1000, this is a classic Orthodox church in the Byzantine style. It's square and topped with a central dome—quite different from Western churches that are long and narrow—with windows of slender columns supporting tall arches. The walls are made of

Rituals of the Eastern Orthodox Church

While the doctrine of Catholic and Orthodox churches remains very similar, many of the rituals are different. As you enter any Greek Orthodox church, you can join in the standard routine: Drop a coin in the wooden box, pick up a candle, say a prayer, light the candle, and place it in the candelabra. Make the sign of the cross and kiss the icon.

Rather than a table-like altar, Orthodox churches come with an **altar screen** (the iconostasis) covered with curtains, dividing the lay community from the priests—the material world from the spiritual one. Worshippers stand through the service as a sign of respect (though some older parishioners sit on the seats along the walls). Traditionally, women stand on the left side, men on the right (equal distance from the altar, to represent that all are equal before God).

The Orthodox faith tends to use a Greek **cross,** with four equal arms (like a plus sign), which focuses on God's perfection; the longer Latin cross used by Catholics more literally evokes the Crucifixion.

Orthodox **icons** (golden paintings of saints) are not intended to be lifelike. Packed with intricate symbolism and often cast against a shimmering golden background, they're meant to remind viewers of the metaphysical nature of Jesus and the saints rather than their physical form, which is considered irrelevant.

Most Eastern Orthodox churches have at least one mosaic or painting of Christ in a standard pose—as **Pantocrator,** a Greek word meaning "All Powerful." The image, so familiar to Orthodox Christians, shows Christ as King of the Universe, facing directly out, with penetrating eyes. Behind his head is a halo divided by a cross—a symbol for the Crucifixion, hinting of the Resurrection and salvation that follow.

Orthodox services generally involve **chanting**—a dialogue between the priest and the congregation. The church is filled with the evocative aroma of incense, heightening the ambience. Each of these ritual elements does its part to help the worshipper transcend the physical world and enter into communion with the spiritual one.

brick and mortar, with large blocks scavenged from earlier buildings incorporated into it.

Make your way to the entrance. Over the door is a mosaic of Mary and baby Jesus on a gold background. Though modern, this maintains the traditional rigid style of so many icons.

Church of Kapnikarea—"icon"-ic Orthodox in the middle of trendy Ermou street

Inside the Church: If the church is open, step inside. You're welcome to visit, as long as you're modestly dressed, keep your voice low, and don't take photos.

In the narrow entryway, notice the bank of candles, and observe the standard routine (see the sidebar). You may notice lipstick smudges on the protective glass. The icon gets changed with a different saint according to the church calendar. Also notice the candle-recycling box behind the candelabra.

Explore deeper into the main part of the church. Find the typical Orthodox features: The nave is basically square and symmetrical, with four equal arms radiating out from the dome. The decoration is pretty sparse: icons on the walls, a wooden pulpit, a few hanging lamps, and a handful of chairs.

The focus of the church is the white-marble partition—the iconostasis. During the service, the priest goes through the iconostasis' doorway, into the inner sanctum, to prepare the eucharist. Notice the four typical icons: Jesus and John the Baptist to the right of the door, and Mary-and-babe to the left, along with a local saint (obscure to most).

Now, look up into the central dome. Looking back at you from

Kapnikarea, with a traditional Byzantine-style mosaic over the door

heaven is Jesus, as Pantocrator ("All Powerful"). He surveys the universe with his penetrating gaze, raises his hand, and gives it his blessing.

▶ *From this humble chapel, let's head to the most important church in the Greek Orthodox world. Walk toward the Acropolis, downhill on Kapnikareas street (to the left as you come down Ermou street). After two blocks turn left on traffic-free Pandrossou street, which leads to the...*

❻ Cathedral (Mitropolis)

This is the "Greek Vatican"—the home church of the archbishop who presides over the country's 10 million Orthodox Christians. It's the city's cathedral, or (in Greek), its "metropolitan" church. It's probably flying the blue-and-white Greek flag, because it's the national church.

Though the structure is relatively modern (built in 1842), it has many typical Byzantine-style features, like tall windows, horseshoe arches, and a glittering mosaic of the Annunciation.

Inside the Church: You'll find the same features found in all Orthodox churches but on a grander scale. Notice the balconies. In past times, this was where women worshipped. But in 1954, Greek women got the vote, and now they worship alongside the men.

On Cathedral Square: Out front stands a statue of a man with a staff, giving a blessing. This is the honored **Archbishop Damaskinos** (1891-1949), who presided here in the early 20th century. During the Nazi occupation of Greece, he was one of the rare Christian leaders who spoke out on behalf of persecuted Jews. The Nazis threatened to put Damaskinos before a firing squad. The feisty archbishop joked that they should hang him instead, in good Orthodox tradition. After the war, he served as Greece's caretaker prime minister, helping bring stability to the war-torn country. Athens' Jewish community erected this statue as a show of thanks.

The statue depicts many typical Orthodox features. Damaskinos wears the distinctive hat of an Orthodox archbishop—a kind of fez with cloth hanging down the sides. He carries a staff and blesses with his right hand. Look closely at the hand—he's touching his thumb to his ring finger. This is the traditional Orthodox sign of the cross. The gesture forms the letters of the alphabet that spell out the Greek name of Jesus. Try it yourself. Touch your thumb to the tip of your ring finger. Now, your pinkie forms the letter I; your slightly crossed index and middle fingers are an X; and your thumb and ring finger make a double-C. These four letters—I, C, X, C—are short for...Jesus Christ. Very clever. So if you were an Orthodox priest, you'd hold your fingers like this and wave your arm three times, tracing the shape of a cross, and chanting "the Father, the Son, and the Holy Spirit."

Notice Damaskinos' necklace. It's the double-headed eagle of the Byzantine Empire, when Orthodoxy became the state religion. The two heads demonstrated how the Byzantine emperor ruled both

Athens' cathedral—the "Greek Vatican"

Archbishop making the sign of Jesus

Constantine XI couldn't stop the Ottomans.

Agios Eleftherios church, with old stones

East and West, as well as both the secular and the spiritual worlds. The Byzantine Empire dominated Europe for a thousand years, with Athens as one of its premier cities. But then everything changed.

For that, find the statue at the far end of the square—behind Damaskino to the left, farthest from the cathedral. The statue of a warrior holding a sword is **Emperor Constantine XI,** the final ruler of that great Byzantine Empire. In 1453, Emperor Constantine was toppled from power and the great city of Constantinople was conquered by the Ottoman Turks. Almost overnight, Muslims controlled Athens, and Orthodox Christians had to lay low for the next four centuries.

▶ *That's when our next stop came into play in Athens' long history. Head for the small church along the right side of the cathedral. It's the...*

❼ Church of Agios Eleftherios

When the Ottomans took control, they evicted Athens' archbishops from their previous cathedral—the Parthenon, which at that time was used as a church. With the Parthenon now a mosque, the archbishop moved here, to this humble church with a venerable history.

Built in the 12th and 13th centuries, it's dedicated to a popular saint (*agios*). The little church is still referred to as "the old cathedral," since it actually was once the cathedral. (If you go inside, you'll find a mostly bare space with typical features.)

Check out the facade. The church is a jigsaw puzzle of reused stones scavenged from earlier monuments, some of them extremely old. Over the door, the lintel has crosses, lions, and rosettes. A little higher up is a row of carved panels featuring more crosses, griffins and eagles, sphinxes, eagles eating snakes, and ancient floral designs. These date from the second century AD. They were once part of a calendar of pagan Athenian festivals that stood in the Ancient Agora. Even higher, there's a frieze from before the time of Christ, depicting toga-clad men in an ancient parade.

Notice the wide variety of crosses. The Maltese cross has four V-shaped arms. It was popular with Crusaders who passed through here on their way to Jerusalem. The Latin cross has a long base and shorter crossbar, symbolic of the Crucifixion. The one with two crossbars is the Patriarchal Cross, popular with archbishops. The Greek cross has four equal arms, symbolic of God's perfection.

Circle the church (counterclockwise) to find more old stones and symbols, both Christian and pagan. There are even old tombstones. This combination of pagan and Christian elements testifies to Athens' long history, incorporating diverse cultural traditions.

▶ *We're at ground zero of the Greek Orthodox faith. Let's check out a few nearby sights that show off the Orthodox church of today.*

Make your way directly behind the Church of Agios Eleftherios, where there's a row of shops. These shops are along a street called…

❽ Agia Filotheis Street

This neighborhood is a hive of activity for Orthodox clerics. It's home to many stores selling all kinds of religious objects. The Orthodox religion comes with its own unique religious paraphernalia, from robes to incense burners, candelabras to icons. **Crown Church Supplies** (at #5) is a family-run business that's been tailoring robes for Orthodox priests since 1907.

Turn right and explore more of Agia Filotheis street. Cross busy Apollonos street and go another 30 yards to #15 Agia Filotheis street, on the left. Explore these **stoas** (mini malls) with several workshops of local artisans who make religious objects. You may see painters at work creating or restoring icons. Or tailors fashioning bishops' robes. Or metalworkers creating gold lamps and chalices exquisitely worked in elaborate repoussé design.

In this neighborhood, keep an eye out for Orthodox priests. They dress all in black, wear beards, and don those fez-like hats. While they look like celibate monks, most are husbands and fathers. Married priests are welcome, as long as they marry before becoming priests. They're generally well-educated pillars of the community, serving as counselors and spiritual guides to the cosmopolitan populace.

A little farther along (on the left) is the cute little **Church of Agia**

Filotheis, named for one of the patron saints of Athens. This garden church is a popular place for weddings. A few steps farther (at #19, on the left) is an impressive marble building with a golden double eagle on the facade and busts of bishops out front. Note the heightened security. This is the official **residence of the archbishop** of Athens.

▶ *At this point, our walk focuses on...*

Part 3: Athens' "Old Town" (The Plaka and Anafiotika)

This part of our walk explores the atmospheric twisty lanes of old Athens. Here we'll find some of Athens' oldest monuments, dating back to ancient times. These days, the neighborhood called the Plaka is both atmospheric and very touristy.

▶ *Continue up Agia Filotheis street a few more yards until you reach a tight five-way intersection. Turn right, then left, heading uphill on Adrianou street (labeled Αδριανού)—choked with souvenir stands and tourists.*

❾ Adrianou Street

This intersection may be the geographical—if not atmospheric—center of the Plaka. Touristy Adrianou street is the main pedestrian drag, cutting through the neighborhood.

We'll walk about 200 yards up Adrianou street to where it dead ends. As you walk, you'll be running the full gauntlet of Greek souvenirs—sea sponges, olive oil, icons, and tacky T-shirts that say "Got Ouzo?" There are also plenty of cafés seemingly designed for tired tourists.

And what's with all the worry beads for sale? They range from cheap glass beads to authentic hand-cut amber. Greeks endlessly fondle and twirl these strings of beads. Worry beads may be based on religious beads used to keep track of prayers, like Catholics use the rosary or Muslims use prayer beads. But today's worry beads have no religious overtones—they're used to relieve anxiety and get focused. Traditionally, only men used worry beads, but they're becoming increasingly popular among Greek women as well.

▶ *Window-shop your way gently uphill until you reach the T-intersection with Lysikratous street.*

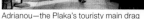

| Adrianou—the Plaka's touristy main drag | Hadrian's arch marks the Roman conquest. |

We now turn our attention to some of Athens' oldest monuments, from the ancient days when it was one of the greatest cities on earth. (To get in an ancient mood, check out the excavation site amid the trees nearby, showing the level of the street 2,000 years ago.)

Looking left, down Lysikratous street, you can see our next stop—the Arch of Hadrian. (If your fuel gauge is running low, you could skip the Arch of Hadrian and the Temple of Olympian Zeus, and jump ahead to the Lysicrates Monument, which is just a few steps to your right.)

To continue the walk, head down Lysikratous street, cross busy Vasilissis Amalias avenue (crosswalk nearby), and approach the...

⑩ Arch of Hadrian and Temple of Olympian Zeus

In 146 BC, Athens came under the control of the growing Roman Empire. But the Romans—who loved Greek culture, architecture, and statues—only made the city greater. Athens' best benefactor was the great Grecophile Emperor Hadrian (or, as he was known in Greece, Adrianou). He built an enormous planned neighborhood known as—what else?—Hadrianopolis.

The **Arch of Hadrian**—a classic triumphal arch in the Roman style—marked the entrance to the emperor's planned community. The arch was once brilliant white, made of the same Pentelic marble as the Parthenon. It's now stained by exhaust from some of Athens' worst traffic. The arch is topped with Corinthian columns, with their leafy capitals. Corinthian was the Greek style preferred by the Romans. Hadrian built the arch in 132 AD to mark the line between Greek Athens and the new Roman city. An inscription on the west side (facing Vasilissis Amalias) reads, "This is Athens, ancient city of Theseus." The opposite frieze says, "This is the city of Hadrian, and not of Theseus." This arch must have been a big deal for Hadrian, as the emperor himself came here to celebrate the inauguration.

Now look past the arch to see the huge—and I mean huge—Corinthian columns. This is all that remains of the **Temple of Olympian Zeus** (entrance is a 5-minute walk to the left, circling the fence clockwise). This was the largest temple in ancient Greece and took almost 700 years to complete. It was begun in the sixth century BC by the Greeks, then lay abandoned, half-built, for centuries. Finally, Hadrian finished the job in 131 AD.

The temple was huge. Those Corinthian columns are a towering 56 feet high. Compare that with the 34-foot-high columns of the puny Parthenon. The finished temple was 360 feet long by 145 feet wide. It was the size of a football field, or more than twice the square footage of the Parthenon.

The Temple of Olympian Zeus had 104 columns—two rows of 20 columns on each of the long sides and three rows of eight columns along each end. Only 15 columns remain standing. The fallen column you see—like a tipped-over stack of bottle caps—was knocked over by a storm in 1852. This over-the-top temple was dedicated to Zeus, who lived on Mount Olympus. The temple contained two enormous statues: one of the ruler of the gods—Zeus—and an equally colossal statue of the ruler of the Greeks...Hadrian.

▶ *Let's delve even deeper into Athens' past, as we make our way to the Acropolis.*

Backtrack up Lysikratous street to where we were earlier, at the T-intersection. Just uphill from that intersection, Lysikratous street spills out into a small, leafy square with the Acropolis rising above it. In the square is a round, white monument.

⑪ Lysicrates Monument and Square

The elegant marble Lysicrates monument has Corinthian columns that support a dome topped with a (rather damaged) statue. Check out the frieze around the top portion. You may be able to see that it represents Dionysus turning pirates into dolphins.

The monument is the sole survivor of many such monuments that once lined this street. This was the ancient "Street of the Tripods," so-called because the monuments came with bronze tripods alongside. These three-legged stands (like those you'll see in the museums) held trophies—things like ornamental vases and cauldrons. Here on

At the Temple of Olympian Zeus, the Romans used Greek styles to build on a colossal scale.

Lysicrates Monument—an ancient "Oscar"

Lykavittos Hill, seen from the Acropolis

this street, the ancient "Oscars" were awarded to winners of theatrical competitions staged at the nearby Theater of Dionysus. The Lysicrates Monument honors one of the winners—the winning choral team from the year 334 BC. Excavations around the monument have uncovered the foundations of other monuments, which are now reburied under a layer of red sand, awaiting further study.

Now stroll the square itself. Shaded by trees, this is a pleasant place to take a break before we climb the hill. Have a coffee at one of the café tables, or try a frappé—an iced coffee with foam. Or you can pop into the hole-in-the-wall grocery store to the left, and grab a cheap cold drink from the cooler, and sit for free on the benches under the trees.

▶ *When you're ready to move on, find the Epimenidou staircase on the left side of the square (near the grocery store), and start climbing. At the top of the stairs, the street leads left to the Acropolis Museum and south entrance gate, but for now we'll turn right, which leads around the lower flanks of...*

⑫ Acropolis Hill

As you walk (past olive trees), you're treading the same paths followed by humans since the beginning of recorded time. From cave dwellers to modern man, Athenians have lived on, around, or in the shadow of this hill. The Acropolis—or "high city"—has been the heart of Athens since the Neolithic era, around 7000 BC. The sheer plateau was a natural fortress—faced with 100-foot cliffs, and fed by permanent springs.

Acropolis hill is a limestone ridge that's flat on top. Its footprint covers seven acres. The Mycenaeans built the first palaces on top (around 1400 BC), and their Greek descendants built temples to their patron goddess Athena (around 800 BC). When the Persians destroyed all of the Acropolis' temples (480 BC), it left a blank canvas. The resilient Greeks built the Parthenon, ushering in the Golden Age. And for 2,500 years, the grand structures atop this hill have inspired the Western world.

▶ *You'll reach the small **Church of St. George of the Rock** (Agios Georgios), where there's a fork in the road. Go uphill, along the left fork. You'll soon be immersed in a maze of tiny, whitewashed houses. This charming "village" is the neighborhood called...*

⑬ Anafiotika

As you enter the narrow lanes, don't worry about getting lost. Just keep following signs that point to *Acropolis*—even if the path seems impossibly narrow. You'll eventually emerge on the other side.

The tiny homes cling to the hillside, built into and around the Acropolis' craggy outcroppings. This neighborhood of Anafiotika was built by people from the tiny Cycladic island of Anafi, who came to Athens looking for work after Greece gained its independence from the Ottomans. (Many stoneworkers and builders hired to construct the modern city of Athens built these higgledy-piggledy residences after-hours.) Some descendants of the original islanders still live here in Anafiotika ("little Anafi"). Posters of Anafi still hang here and there, evoking the sandy beaches of the ancestral home island. But it's slowly becoming a place for wealthy locals to keep an "island cottage" right here in the city.

Keep following those *Acropolis* signs. Weave through narrow paths, lined with flowers and dotted with cats, dozing peacefully in the sunshine or slithering luxuriously past your legs. In this delightful spot, nestled beneath the walls of the Acropolis, the big city seems a world away. Notice the male fig trees—they're the ones with no fruit, so they keep away flies and mosquitoes. Smell the chicken-manure fertilizer, peek into delicate little yards, and enjoy the blue doors and maroon shutters. It's a transplanted Cycladic Island world.

As you gaze out over the rooftops of modern Athens below, keep an eye out for **views of Lykavittos Hill,** the cone-shaped mound in the distance. It's the highest hill in Athens, topped with a tiny white church at just over 900 feet above sea level. By comparison, the Acropolis is only 490 feet tall. The Lykavittos summit, which can be reached by a funicular, has a restaurant and view terrace. Although it looms high over the cityscape, Lykavittos Hill will always be over-shadowed by the hill you're climbing now.

From the Acropolis—Athens' oldest sight—our walk starts making its way back to the modern world.

▶ *Follow the* Acropolis *signs, through the narrow walkways, until you emerge from the maze of houses at a T-intersection with a wider, cob-bled lane. Turn right (downhill) and continue on the cobbled lane past the neighborhood church tucked around the corner to the right (peek through the metal gate into the festively adorned courtyard). After 50 yards, turn left on a wider road (Theorias), and walk toward the small stone Church of the Metamorphosis. (Note: To reach the Acropo-lis main entrance from here, you would continue along this road as it bends left around the hill. For now, though, let's continue our walk.)*

Just before the church (near the sign for the Athens University His-tory Museum), turn right and go down the steep, narrow staircase called Klepsidras. Go 100 yards down the stairs (past cute homes, in-teresting graffiti, the free little museum, and the recommended Klep-sidra Café), until the staircase dead-ends at a railing overlooking some ruins.

⑭ Roman Forum and Tower of the Winds

The rows of columns framing this rectangular former piazza were built by the Romans. This square was the commercial center, or fo-rum, of Roman Athens. The columns supported a covered porch providing shade for shoppers browsing the many stores fronting the square. Picture this place filled with Roman bureaucrats and Greek locals. The forum—or open-air piazza—was a feature found in every city Rome conquered. Here, it was dotted with Greek-style buildings and statues. Like Americans in Paris, Romans relished living in so-phisticated Athens, sprinkling their Latin conversations with Greek phrases as they discussed the plays of Sophocles and Aristophanes. It's possible to enter the Roman Forum for a closer look at the rubble (the entrance is on the west end) but you can see just about everything from here (for more on what's inside, see page 138).

Now, take a few steps to the right for a closer look at the octago-nal, domed **Tower of the Winds.** Built in the first century BC, this building was an ingenious combination of clock, weather station, and guide to the planets. The tower was once capped with a weathervane in the form of a bronze Triton—half-man, half-fish. Bronze rods (no longer visible) protruded from the walls and acted as sundials to indicate the time. And when the sun wasn't shining, people told time using the tower's sophisticated water clock inside, powered by water piped in from springs on the Acropolis. Much later, under Ottoman rule, dervishes used the tower as a place for their whirling worship and prayer.

Look closely at the tower's carved reliefs. They depict the traditional eight winds of the world as winged angels, who fly in, bringing the weather. Find the weather-angel holding the curved rudder of a ship—he's the wind who brings good sailing weather. The next relief (to the right) shows an angel turning an urn upside down, spilling out rain.

To see more reliefs, circle the Tower counterclockwise, as we make our way downhill to our next destination. As you turn the corner, find the old bearded man wrapping his cloak up tight against the cold weather. On the Tower's right side is an angel with a robe full of fruit, bringing the abundance of summer. Next (as you continue circling counterclockwise), an angel with a round shield is about to dump out hailstones. Finally (at the downhill side of the Tower), find the north wind, wearing a heavy robe and blowing on a conch shell to usher in winter.

From this vantage point, you can look through the fence into the Roman Forum. Find some rectangular ruins surrounded by a wider rectangular ditch—the ancient forum's public restroom.

▶ *By now you should be at the downhill side of the Tower of the Winds. Facing the Tower, turn 180 degrees, and find the start of narrow Aiolou (Αιολоу) street. Head downhill on Aiolou street one block, where it opens up into the leafy, restaurant-filled...*

Roman Forum, heart of Roman Athens

Tower of the Winds, with carved reliefs

⓯ Agora Square (Plateia Agoras)

This square is the touristy epicenter of the Plaka. On the left side of the square you'll see the second-century AD ruins of the ⓰ **Library of Hadrian,** built by that Greek-loving Roman emperor, Hadrian, for the good of his beloved Athens. Four lone columns sit atop apse-like foundations. The ruins around it are all that's left of a big rectangular complex that once boasted 100 marble columns. It was a huge cultural center, with a library, lecture halls, garden, and art gallery. Notice how the excavated stones rest neatly in stacks awaiting funding for reconstruction.

▶ *We're on the home stretch now. Continue downhill alongside the ruins one block, and turn left onto* ⓱ ***Pandrossou street**—a narrow lane choked with souvenir shops. Expert pickpockets work this crowded lane—be careful. Continue until you spill out into Monastiraki Square.*

⓲ Monastiraki Square Spin-Tour

We've made it from Syntagma Square—the center of urban Athens—to the city's *other* main square, Monastiraki Square, the gateway to the touristy Old Town. To get oriented to Monastiraki Square, stand in the center, face the small church with the cross on top (which is north), and pan clockwise.

The name Monastiraki ("Little Monastery") refers to this square, the surrounding neighborhood, the flea-market action near-by...and the cute **Church of the Virgin** in the square's center (12th-century Byzantine, mostly restored with a much more modern bell tower).

Beyond the church (straight ahead from the end of the square), **Athinas street** heads north to the Central Market, Omonia Square, and (after about a mile) the National Archaeological Museum.

Just to the right (behind the little church) is the head of **Ermou street**—the bustling shopping drag we walked down earlier. If you turned right and walked straight up Ermou, you'd be back at Syntagma Square in 10 minutes.

Next (on the right, in front of the little church) comes Mitropoleos street—Athens' **"Souvlaki Row."** Clogged with outdoor tables, this at-mospheric lane is home to a string of restaurants that serve sausage-shaped, skewered meat—grilled up spicy and tasty. The place on the corner—Bairaktaris (Μπαϊρακταρησ)—is the best known, its walls

Leafy Agora Square, lined with eateries

Souvlaki Row—for a cheap, filling meal

lined with photos of famous politicians and artists who come here for souvlaki and pose with the owner. But the other two joints along here—Thanasis and Savas—have a better reputation for their souvlaki. You can sit at the tables, or, for a really cheap meal, order a souvlaki to go. A few blocks farther down Mitropoleos is the cathedral we visited earlier.

Continue spinning clockwise. Just past Pandrossou street (where you entered the square), you'll see a **former mosque** (look for the Arabic script under the portico and over the wooden door). Known as the Tzami (from the Turkish word for "mosque"), this was a place of worship when Athens was under Ottoman rule (15th-19th centuries).

To the right of the mosque, behind the fence along Areos street, you might glimpse some huge Corinthian columns. This is the opposite end of the **Library of Hadrian** complex we saw earlier. Areos street stretches up toward the Acropolis. If you were to walk a block up this street, then turn right on Adrianou, you'd reach the ⓳ **Ancient Agora**—one of Athens' top ancient attractions (for more, see the 📖 Ancient Agora Tour chapter or download my free 🎧 audio tour). Beyond the Agora are the delightful Thissio neighborhood, ancient Keramikos Cemetery, and Gazi district.

As you continue panning clockwise, next comes the pretty yellow building that houses the **Monastiraki Metro station.** This was Athens' original, 19th-century train station—Neoclassical with a dash of Byzantium. This bustling Metro stop is now the intersection of two lines: the old line 1 (green, with connections to the port of Piraeus, the Thissio neighborhood, and Victoria—near the National

Flea market chairs, for a well-deserved rest

Archaeological Museum) and the modern line 3 (blue, with connections to Syntagma Square and the airport).

Just right of the station, Ifestou street leads downhill into the **flea market** (antiques, jewelry, cheap clothing, and so on), plus the interesting **TAF Foundation** art-collective/bar set in a traditional Athenian house.

Keep panning clockwise. Just beyond busy Ermou street (behind the A for Athens hotel—which has a rooftop bar popular for its views) is the happening ㉔ **Psyrri** district. For years a run-down slum, this zone is being gentrified by twentysomethings with a grungy sense of style. Packed with cutting-edge bars, boutique hotels, restaurants, cafés, and nightclubs, it may seem foreboding and ramshackle, but it is actually fun to explore.

This walk has taken us through 2,500 years of Athens' history—though in reverse order. We've ended on a bustling square where Athens—both old and new—comes together. Explore and enjoy this global capital—the springboard of so much Western civilization, and the place that more than one in three Greeks call home.

▶ *Our walk is over. If you've worked up an appetite, savor a spicy souvlaki on "Souvlaki Row" or eat your way through the local and colorful Psyrri neighborhood (see the Eating chapter for recommendations).*

Ancient Agora Tour

Αρχαία Αγορά

While the Acropolis was the ceremonial showpiece, the Agora was the real heart of ancient Athens. For some 800 years (c. 600 BC–AD 300), it was the place where people came to shop, businessmen struck deals, laws were passed, worshippers venerated the gods, and theaters hummed with nightlife. Agora means "gathering place," and this was a lively place where the pace never let up—much like modern Athens.

Little survives from the classical Agora. Other than one very well-preserved temple and a rebuilt stoa, it's a field of humble ruins. But that makes it a quiet, uncrowded spot to wander and get a feel for the ancients. Nestled in the shadow of the Acropolis, it's an ideal prelude to your visit there.

ORIENTATION

Cost: €8, covered by €30 Acropolis combo-ticket (which you can buy here; see sidebar on page 135).

Hours: Daily 8:00-20:00, Oct until 18:00, Nov-March until 15:00. The Agora Museum inside generally has the same hours.

Information: Tel. 210-321-0180, http://odysseus.culture.gr.

Getting There: From the Monastiraki Metro stop, walk a block south (uphill, toward the Acropolis). Turn right on Adrianou street, and follow the pedestrian-only, café-lined street along the railroad tracks for about 200 yards. The Agora entrance is on your left, across from a small, yellow church. The entrance can be hard to spot: It's where a path crosses over the railroad tracks (look for a small, pale-yellow sign that says *Ministry of Culture—Ancient Agora*).

Visitor Information: Panels with printed descriptions of the ruins are scattered helpfully throughout the site.

Tours: ∩ Download my free Ancient Agora audio tour.

WCs: The only WCs are inside the Stoa of Attalos, at its northernmost end.

Eating: Picnicking is not allowed in the Agora. Loads of cafés and tavernas line busy Adrianou street near the entrance, and more good eateries front the Apostolou Pavlou pedestrian walkway that hems in the western edge of the Agora, in the district called Thissio.

Starring: A well-preserved temple, a rebuilt stoa with a nice museum, some monumental statues, and the ruins of the civilization that built the Western world.

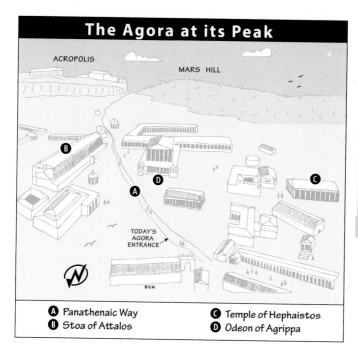

The Agora at its Peak

ACROPOLIS

MARS HILL

B

D

A

TODAY'S
AGORA
ENTRANCE

C

DCH

A Panathenaic Way   **C** Temple of Hephaistos
B Stoa of Attalos   **D** Odeon of Agrippa

THE TOUR BEGINS

Entering the site from Adrianou street, belly up to the illustration at the top of the ramp that shows the Athenian Agora at the peak of its size. Face the Acropolis (to the south) and look out over the expanse of ruins and trees. This overgrown field was once the center of Athenian life.

Get oriented. You're standing near #26 on the illustration (not #28, as it confusingly implies). At your feet runs the Panathenaic Way (#21), the Agora's main street, then and now. The long column-lined building to the left is the reconstructed Stoa of Attalos (#13). To your right (though likely obscured by trees) is the Temple of Hephaistos (#20). Directly ahead of you (through more trees) are the remains of the Odeon of Agrippa (#12).

Panathenaic Way cutting through the Agora   Statue-columns amid the greenery

In the distance, the Agora's far end is bordered by hills. From left to right are the Acropolis (#1), the Areopagus ("Hill of Ares," or Mars Hill, #2), and Pnyx Hill (#3).

The place where you're standing was near the Altar of the Twelve Gods, which was once considered the geographical center of Athens, from which distances were measured. You've arrived at ground zero of ancient Athens.

▶ *Walk to the bottom of the ramp at your left to the path that was once Athens' main street. Find a shady spot to ponder ancient Athenian life in its heyday.*

❶ The Panathenaic Way—the Agora in its Prime

Imagine walking through the Agora along its main drag in ancient times.

On your left stood the Stoa of Attalos, which looked much like this modern reconstruction today. On your right was the Agora's main square, surrounded by gleaming, white-marble buildings. Everywhere you looked there were temples, government buildings, and theaters, all fronted with columns and topped with red-tile roofs. The place was studded with trees and dotted with statues, fountains, and altars. The streets were lined with wooden market stalls where merchants sold produce, pottery, and trinkets.

The Agora buzzed with people, day and night. Imagine men and women dressed in their simple tunics. They came to shop—to buy groceries, clothes, painted plates and pitchers, or to get their wagon wheel fixed. If you needed a zoning permit for your business, you came to the courthouse. Worshippers gave offerings to the gods at any number of

Ancient Agora

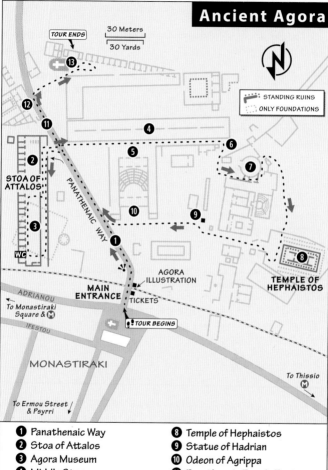

30 Meters
30 Yards

TOUR ENDS

STANDING RUINS
ONLY FOUNDATIONS

STOA OF ATTALOS

PANATHENAIC WAY

WC

ADRIANOU
To Monastiraki Square & Ⓜ
IFESTOU

MAIN ENTRANCE

AGORA ILLUSTRATION

TICKETS

TOUR BEGINS

TEMPLE OF HEPHAISTOS

MONASTIRAKI

To Thissio Ⓜ

To Ermou Street / & Psyrri

1 Panathenaic Way
2 Stoa of Attalos
3 Agora Museum
4 Middle Stoa
5 Corinthian Capital
6 Great Drain
7 Tholos
8 Temple of Hephaistos
9 Statue of Hadrian
10 Odeon of Agrippa
11 Panathenaic Parade Route
12 Post-Herulian Wall
13 Church of the Holy Apostles

temples and altars. At night, people came for plays and concerts. The tavernas rocked.

The Panathenaic Way started at the main city gate, cut diagonally through the Agora's main square, and wound its way up to the Acropolis—two-thirds of a mile in all. This was the city's main north-south road, and here in the Agora it intersected with the main east-west road to the busy port of Piraeus. Though some stretches were paved, most of it (then as now) was just packed gravel.

All roads led to the Agora. This was the place for speeches, political announcements, celebrations, and demonstrations. On holidays, the parade ran right up this street. At any time, this was the place to be—to run into eccentric characters like Socrates or Diogenes, or just to hang out with friends. In short, this was the buzzing center of the city of Athens, population 100,000.

▶ *Now turn your attention to the long, colonnaded building on your left. The entrance is at the far (south) end. Step onto its shaded porch, look down the long rows of columns, and admire the...*

❷ Stoa of Attalos

This stoa was an ancient shopping mall. Covered walkways like this protected shoppers from the sun and the rain. The ground floor once had about 20 shops—today, those rooms hold the museum. Upstairs were offices, which today house the American School.

The stoa was originally built around 150 BC by King Attalos II of Pergamon (in modern-day Turkey). Though he was not a Greek, Attalos was—like so many other ancient people—fascinated by Greek culture. This building was his way of saying thanks for the education he'd received in Athens. The original structure is long gone, but the building that stands today is a faithful reconstruction, built in the 1950s by the American School of Classical Studies, which helped excavate the Agora.

This stoa is typical of many others in ancient Athens. It stands two stories tall, and was made of white Pentelic marble, the same as the Parthenon. The covered porch is about 400 feet long. It's lined with one row of 45 Doric columns (the outer layer) and another row of 22 Ionic columns—a typical mixing of styles.

The statues on display in the arcade once populated the Agora—gods, heroes, athletes, and ceremonial *stele*. For example, on the wall

Stoa of Attalos—reconstructed "mall"

The stoa now houses the Agora Museum.

near the fifth Ionic column, find the impressive sculpted head of a bearded man with a full head of hair. This Head of a Triton (c. 150 AD) once decorated the Odeon of Agrippa, which we'll see later.

▶ *About halfway down the arcade you'll find the entrance to the Agora Museum (included with your ticket).*

❸ Agora Museum

The Agora itself is mostly ruins, but the excellent little museum displays some choice rubble that helps bring the place back to life. Start in the corner, with a photo from 1952 showing this spot before the stoa was reconstructed—just a long platform.

This long hall is laid out chronologically, letting you trace the history of the Agora through artifacts (mainly pottery) found here. Follow the collection by the numbers found in the display cases' upper right corner. The cases are rather confusingly labeled but easy to find.

▶ *The first cases chart the rise of the Agora from a tiny settlement to the center of enlightened Golden Age Athens.*

Case #1 (center of the room): This reclining female figure dates from the Agora's first inhabitants, way back around 4,000 BC, who found a home in this rectangular-shaped valley in the protective shadow of the Acropolis.

#8 (right wall): These tomb offerings came from the next settlers: the Mycenaeans (c. 1600-1200 BC), who built atop the Acropolis and used the Agora as a cemetery.

#9 (right): This handsome vase (with its intricate patterns, symmetrical designs, and stick figures) is, not surprisingly, from the Geometric period (1100-700 BC). Its presence indicates that the Agora now had permanent residents and pottery workshops.

An ancient commode

Clay ballot voting Aristides out of Athens

#3 (center): As Athens grew, the pottery got more sophisticated, depicting increasingly realistic humans and animals. During this Archaic era (700-500 BC) the Agora expanded, got its first monumental buildings, and hosted its first Panathenaic parade.

#26 (right): Yes, it's just what it looks like—a baby's commode. It dates from the time when the Agora was still largely a residential neighborhood, rather than the all-commercial "downtown" it would become.

#4 (center): This bust of Nike (which means Victory) celebrates Athens' triumph over Persia, when it rebuilt the Agora, ushered in the Golden Age (roughly 480-400 BC), and established a flourishing democracy.

▶ *The next several displays are devoted to one of Athens' greatest inventions—democracy.*

#30 (right): The pottery shards with names painted on them were voter ballots (called *ostrakon*) used to vote out—or ostracize—corrupt tyrants. On the two shards, #37 and #17, read the Greek names—Themistocles and Aristides (ΘΕΜΙΣΘΟΚΛΕΣ ΝΕΟΚΛΕΟΣ and ΑΡΙΣΣΤΕΙΔΕΣ). During the Golden Age, these men were famous rivals, in both politics and romance. Both served Athens honorably and both were also exiled in political power struggles.

#31 (right): This contraption is an early voting machine called the *kleroterion*. It was used to select city council members. It was done randomly, to make sure each citizen fulfilled their civic duty—kind of like jury duty. Citizens put their name in the slots, then black and white balls went into the tube (on the left) to randomly select who would serve. Now look below the machine—you'll see actual bronze ballots from the fourth century.

#32 (right): The *klepsydra* ("water thief") was a water clock used to time speeches at council meetings. It took six minutes for the 1.7 gallons to drain out.

#67 (left): The bronze shield was captured from defeated Spartans in the tide-turning Battle of Sphacteria, which gave Athens the upper hand in the Peloponnesian War. The victory was only temporary, and Athens drained itself in those wars with Sparta.

Just to the left of case #67 is the "Stele of Democracy." A relief carving shows Lady Democracy crowning a man representing the Athenian people. The inscription proclaims that all tyranny is outlawed. Note the monument's date: from around 336 BC, the year Alexander the Great took control of Greece and began spreading Greek culture throughout the known world.

▶ *The final exhibits date from the Agora's later years, when it was the center of a large, multicultural, cosmopolitan Hellenistic world.*

#66 (left): These marble "herm" heads of prominent men stood atop columns that were placed at major intersections. They warded off evil spirits and were signposts, with the latest news and directions attached.

#34 and **#35** (right): Pottery was a popular export product for the sea-trading Greeks. The sophisticated Athenians set the trends—from black figures painted on a red background (case #34) to red on black (case #35).

#5 (center): In the middle of the room is a case of coins. These drachms and tetradrachms feature Athena with her helmet. In Golden Age times, a drachm was roughly a day's wage. The ancients put coins like these in the mouth of a deceased person as payment to carry the soul safely across the River Styx. Coin #7, a four-drachm piece, features the owl as on Greece's €1 coin today.

#58 and **#56** (left): These sculpture heads date from the Agora's next great era, the Romans. The Romans loved Greek culture and expanded the Agora, leaving many of the ruins seen today. As these busts show, the Romans were more honest than the Greeks when it came to portraying people with less-than-ideal features.

#55 (far end): After the decline of Rome, the Agora suffered, but—as these fine, intricately patterned pieces of Byzantine pottery attest—it still shone on. The Agora was a vital neighborhood of Athens until 1204, when invading Venetians sacked and looted it, and the Agora was abandoned...leaving all these artifacts in the rubble, waiting for archaeologists to retrieve them and build this museum.

▸ *To reach the stoa's upper floor, exit this room and turn right into the arcade, passing a WC and water fountain. At the far end, find the stairway leading up to the second level.*

Upper Stoa: From here in the open-air upper stoa, you have great views down into the Agora and across to the Temple of Hephaistos. Halfway down the hall, focus on the model of the Agora at its peak of grandeur, under the Romans, in the second century AD. Find the long, low building behind the odeon. This was another stoa—the Middle Stoa. That's where we're headed next.

▸ *Go back downstairs, return to the spot where we first entered, and head across the Panathenaic Way. Continue straight (west) along the lane and across the middle of the Agora. You're walking alongside the vast ruins (on your left) of what once was the...*

❹ Middle Stoa

This long set of ruins—about 500 feet long by 60 feet wide—stretches clear across the Agora. It served as a big mall of shops and offices for busy Athens. Remember that, during the Golden Age, this central part of the Agora was just an open field, a "gathering place." But as Athens grew and expanded, so did its commercial center. The Middle Stoa (180 BC) was one of several grand buildings that began to fill the space. Eventually it became jam-packed with big marble buildings—the maze of ruins you see today.

▸ *Midway down the lane (near the wooden section of the path), you'll come across a huge capital of a column.*

❺ Corinthian Capital

This capital once stood here atop a colossal column. Carved in the fourth century BC, this is one of the earliest examples of the style known as Corinthian. The Corinthian order featured slender, fluted columns topped with leafy capitals like this. The style was actually rarely used by Greeks, but it became wildly popular with the Romans. When the Romans occupied Athens, they incorporated older Greek capitals like this one into their massive theater. You can see the ruins of that theater (Odeon of Agrippa) as you look toward the Agora entrance.

This leaf-ornamented Corinthian capital once topped a column at the Roman-built Odeon.

▶ *But we're getting ahead of ourselves. Continue westward across the Agora. Near the end of the Middle Stoa, you'll see a gray wellhead—still in its original spot and worn by the grooves of ropes.*

Just beyond the well to the right, you'll spy a round platform—the tholos. Make your way there—after passing the wooden bridge and turning left, you'll cross over a ditch that was once part of the...

❻ Great Drain

This ditch was part of Athens' impressive waterworks system. It was dug in the fifth century BC and still functions today. The ditch captures rainwater runoff from the southern hills and channels it through the Agora. At this point, two main collection ditches meet and join. If you look closely, you can see exposed parts of the stone-lined ditch. The well we just saw was also part of this water system.

▶ *But the real center of Greek democracy is just a few steps away. It's that round footprint with a stubby column in its center. This is the...*

❼ Tholos

This rotunda-shaped building housed Athens' rulers. It was built around 465 BC, right at the dawn of the Golden Age and of Athenian democracy. About 60 feet across, this round structure was originally ringed with six Ionic columns and topped with a cone-shaped roof.

The *tholos* was the center of Athenian government. It was the headquarters, offices, and meeting hall for the city's 50 ministers. They also lived and ate here, since the law required that at least a third of these ministers be on the premises at all times. The *tholos* housed the official weights and measures. By law, any shopper in the Agora could stop in here and use these to check whether a butcher or tailor was shortchanging them.

The 50 ministers were selected from the 500 ministers who met next door in the *bouleterion* (council house). They, in turn, were elected by the foundation of Athenian democracy—the thousands of free adult male citizens.

The *tholos* was also a kind of temple to democratic rule. The altar in the middle—where the broken column is now—once held a flame that was always kept burning. This represented the hearth of the extended "family" that was Athens.

▶ *Our next stop is the big temple atop the ridge. To reach it, climb the stairs to the left and go through the trees, pausing along the way at a* **viewpoint** *with a chart. Continue to the...*

❽ Temple of Hephaistos

One of the best-preserved and most typical of all Greek temples, this is textbook Golden Age architecture. Started in 450 BC—just before the Parthenon—it was built at Athens' peak as part of the massive reconstruction of the Agora after invading Persians destroyed the city (480 BC). But the temple wasn't completed and dedicated until 415 BC, as work stalled when the Greeks started erecting the great buildings of the Acropolis.

This is a classic peristyle temple (like the Parthenon), meaning that the building is surrounded by columns. Also like the Parthenon, it's made of Pentelic marble in the Doric style, part of Pericles' vision of harking back to Athens' austere, solid roots. But the Temple of Hephaistos is only about half the size of the grand Parthenon and with fewer carvings.

Priests would enter from here at the Agora-facing entrance, through the six columns, beneath the covered portico (note the coffered ceiling), into an alcove ringed by three walls (called the *pronaos* or "pre-temple"), before reaching the central hall (*cella*). There they'd worship a large bronze statue of Hephaistos, the blacksmith god, and one of Athena, patroness of Athens and of arts and crafts. According to legend, Hephaistos hit on Athena, she spurned him, he spilled his semen on the ground...and Athens was born. Appropriately, the temple of these crafty gods was originally surrounded by metalworking and pottery workshops.

The carved reliefs are typical of the Greek love of the "contest," depicting legendary battles between heroes, animals, gods, and mythological beasts.

Looking between the six columns, you'll see the inner frieze, with its scenes of Theseus battling Athens' oppressors. (The great mythological hero would eventually slay the bull-headed Minotaur.) These decorations led Athenians to mistakenly believe that the temple once held the remains of Theseus—and to this day, they call it the Theseion.

Take a few steps to the right to view the temple's long side. Like most temples, it was built atop a platform. The temple has six columns on each end, and 13 on the long sides (counting the corners twice). The columns are Doric—with no base and a simple capital—though these columns are fluted (with vertical stripes), which is not as common. The columns were made by stacking seven column drums. The four carvings (metopes) above the columns also depict Theseus's battles. The rest of the metopes are blank—possibly because they were never finished, but maybe because they once held painted frescoes.

If you venture to the temple's rear entrance, you'd find a fine

The well-preserved Temple of Hephaistos

Frieze of centaurs battling humans

Roman emperor Hadrian loved Greek culture.

Triton fronting the Odeon of Agrippa

frieze of the mythological battle when centaurs crashed a wedding of the mortal Lapith tribe. On the temple's other long side, you can make out bullet holes on the crossbeam, a painful reminder of Greece's 1940s civil war.

The temple is remarkably well-preserved. It remained an important place of worship when the Romans arrived, was converted into a church (and given a roof) in the Christian era, and even stayed open under the Muslim Ottomans.

▶ *We now turn to sights from the Roman period—perhaps the greatest era of the Agora's history. Wind your way down the hill (northeast) to the middle of the Agora and find the headless...*

❾ Statue of Hadrian

The Roman Emperor Hadrian ruled Athens around 120 AD, when Rome was at its peak, and Athens was a vital part of the Europe-wide empire. The statue shows Hadrian wearing the typical Roman military uniform, complete with a breastplate and leather skirt. Where Hadrian's belly button would be, find the tiny insignia on the armor. It shows Romulus and Remus, the legendary founders of Rome being suckled by the she-wolf who raised them. Now look who's standing atop the she-wolf—it's Athena.

This symbolized Hadrian's vision—that by conquering Greece, Rome actually saved and supported that great civilization. Hadrian was a true Grecophile and great benefactor of Athens. In fact, if this statue still had its head, you'd see that Hadrian was the first Roman emperor to wear a Greek-style beard. Hadrian was nicknamed Graecula ("The Little Greek") for his love of Greek philosophy, literature, and the handsome teenager Antinous.

▶ *It was under Roman rule that the Agora got one of its best-known structures. Continue on, heading straight down the lane (to the left of Hadrian) and you'll pass three giants on four pedestals, which once guarded the...*

⑩ Odeon of Agrippa

The Odeon of Agrippa was an ancient theater and concert venue. It was once fronted by a line of six colossal statues, which functioned as columns. Of these, only three survive, along with an empty pedestal. The head of a fourth statue is preserved in the Stoa of Attalos—we saw that earlier. Of the statues that remain here, two are meant to be Tritons, with fish tails, while the other monster has the tail of a snake.

The *odeon* was the centerpiece of the Agora during the Roman era, first built under Caesar Augustus (15 BC). It was a popular place, both for the theater-loving Greeks and their Greek-culture-loving Roman masters.

The theater stood two stories tall and was built into the natural slope of the hill. Originally, the main entrance was on the opposite side, near the Middle Stoa (which we saw earlier). Patrons would enter through monumental columns with Corinthian capitals. As they entered from that end, they were at the top row, looking down at the stage, ringed with 20 rows of seats. The place could seat a thousand spectators. Overhead, the glorious roof spanned 82 feet, with no internal support columns. In its heyday, Athenians might have enjoyed lute concerts, poetry readings, and plays by Aristophanes, Euripides, and Sophocles. The less-sophisticated Romans probably flocked here for more lowbrow entertainment.

The giant statues came later. Around 150 AD, the theater's roof collapsed. By now, the center of Athens was moving away from the Agora, and there were already larger theaters elsewhere. So the *odeon* was rebuilt as a smaller lecture hall, of only 500 seats. The entrance was moved to this end, with the six colossal statues standing guard.

▶ *Continue to the main road, where you'll see we've made a loop. Turn right and head toward the Acropolis, walking once again on the Panathenaic Way. This street was on the...*

Walk the Panathenaic Way, the same street strolled by Socrates, Plato, and today's tourists.

⑪ Panathenaic Parade Route

Even as the importance of the Agora declined in later years, the Panathenaic Way remained Athens' traditional main street. Every year in the middle of summer, the city hosted the Panathenaic Festival (a grander version, the Great Panathenaic Festival, happened every four years). This celebrated the birthday of the goddess Athena and, therefore, of the city itself.

The parade started at the city's main gate (located near today's Keramikos Metro stop). Thousands participated—they banged on tambourines and danced in the streets. At the heart of the parade was a float on wheels, carrying the ceremonial wool robe specially woven as a gift for Athena. The parade wound its way through the Agora and up the Acropolis, where the new dress was presented to Athena.

For nearly 800 years, glorious events like this graced the Agora. But Athens' glory days were coming to an end.

▶ *Continue up the Panathenaic Way, past the Stoa of Attalos. Along the left-hand side of the Panathenaic Way are several crude walls and column fragments.*

⑫ Post-Herulian Wall

This wall marks the beginning of the end of classical Athens.

In AD 267, the barbarian Herulians sailed down from the Black Sea and utterly devastated Athens. The crumbling Roman Empire was helpless to protect its provinces. The Herulians burned most of the Agora's buildings to the ground, including the Odeon of Agrippa, leaving the place in ashes.

As soon as the Herulians left, the surviving Athenians began hastily throwing up this wall to keep future invaders at bay. They used anything they could find: rocks, broken columns, statues, frieze fragments, you name it—all thrown together without mortar. They cobbled together a wall 30 feet high and 10 feet thick. Archaeologists recognize pieces scavenged from destroyed buildings, such as the Stoa of Attalos and the Odeon of Agrippa.

Despite this wall, the Agora never really recovered. A few major buildings were rebuilt, notably a university to preserve the knowledge of Socrates, Plato, Aristotle, and company. But the last great Roman Emperor, Justinian, closed that pagan school in AD 529.

Then came more invasions, mainly the Slavs in 580 AD. Athens dwindled, and its few residents settled in other parts of the city. By 700, the Agora had become a virtual ghost town, now located outside the city walls, exposed to bandits and invaders. It was cannibalized by the Athenians themselves as a quarry for precut stones—it's no wonder so little survives today.

▶ *After the barbarians came...the Christians. On the right is the...*

Post-Herulian wall to keep barbarians out

Holy Apostles church adds a Christian layer.

ⓑ Church of the Holy Apostles

This charming little church with the lantern-like dome marks the Agora's revival. It was built around the year 1000, while Athens was under the protection of the Byzantine Empire, ruled from Constantinople. Athens slowly recovered from centuries of invasions and neglect. Like many Christian churches of the period, this one was built atop the ruins of a pagan religious site. In ancient times, this had been a nymphaeum, or temple atop a sacred spring. The new church commemorated St. Paul, who likely converted pagans to Christianity here in the Agora.

This early church was the prototype for later Athenian churches. It has a central dome, with four equal arms radiating out, forming a Greek cross. The windows have the tall horseshoe-shaped arches typical of the Byzantine style. The church was built of large, rectangular blocks of ashlar stone.

Circle around to the entrance (with its jutting entrance hall that unfortunately spoils the original four equal arms). Inside, the windows are in flower and diamond shapes. The church contains some interesting 18th-century frescoes in the Byzantine style and an icon on the altar. The marble altar screen has some pieces missing, leaving wide-open spaces—these frames once held icons. Now stand in the center of the church and look up. At the top of the dome is Christ Pantocrator ("All Powerful"). Images like this must have given Athenians a sense of security in troubled times, knowing their god was overseeing everything.

▶ *End your tour by looking back over the Agora and modern Athens.*

Legacy of the Agora

When Athens came under the control of the Ottomans in the 15th century, the Agora experienced something of a revival. Under the Muslims, Christian churches like the Holy Apostles were tolerated... but taxed. (The decorative pattern of bricks ringing the eaves, shaped like Arabic letters, were added under an Ottoman-era renovation.)

By the 18th century, the Agora had become a flourishing residential district of houses and churches. In the early 20th century, outdoor movies were shown in the Agora.

Then in the 1930s, Greece got serious about preserving its classical heritage. They forced everyone out and demolished everything, except the historic Church of the Holy Apostles, and excavations began.

As the ancient Agora has become a museum, its former city-center functions have moved elsewhere in Athens. The government center is now at Syntagma Square. The marketplace is Athens' Central Market. Nightlife has shifted to the Plaka, Psyrri, and elsewhere. Monastiraki Square has become one of the new urban hubs. And what's replaced the Panathenaic Way as the city's main arterial? I guess that would be the Metro system.

Looking out from this vantage point, realize that the city of Athens has been continuously inhabited for nearly 3,000 years. It was this city that set the tone for all Western civilization to follow. And the cradle of it all was this small patch of land where the people of Athens gathered—the Agora.

Acropolis Tour

Ακρόπολη

Rising above the sprawl of modern Athens, the Acropolis ("high city") is a lasting testament to ancient Athens' glorious Golden Age in the fifth century BC.

Its four major monuments—the Parthenon, Erechtheion, Propylaea, and Temple of Athena Nike—have survived remarkably well given the beating they've taken over the centuries. While the Persians, Ottomans, and Lord Elgin were cruel to the Acropolis in the past, it's now battling acid rain and pollution. Ongoing restoration means you might see some scaffolding, but even that can't detract from the greatness of this sight.

Climbing Acropolis Hill and rambling its ruins, you'll feel like you've journeyed back in time to the birthplace of Western civilization.

Cost: €20 for Acropolis-only ticket; €30 for Acropolis combo-ticket, which covers Athens' other major ancient sites (see page 135). If you buy your combo-ticket ticket elsewhere, you can bypass the ticket booth here.

Hours: Daily 8:00-20:00, Oct until 18:00, Nov-March until 17:00. Hours are subject to change; check locally before planning your day.

Information: Tel. 210-321-4172, http://odysseus.culture.gr.

Crowd-Beating Tips: The place is miserably packed with tour groups from 10:00 to about 12:30 (when you might have to wait up to 45 minutes to get a ticket). Buying a ticket at another sight may save ticket-buying time but doesn't ensure a speedy entry: The worst lines are caused by the bottleneck of people trying to squeeze into the site through the Propylaea gate.

You have two good options: To avoid both crowds and heat, come in the cool morning hours, right when it opens. You'll be leaving just as everyone else is pouring in. Otherwise, I like to visit late in the day—as the sun goes down, the white Parthenon stone gleams a creamy golden brown, and it's suddenly peaceful.

Getting In: The Acropolis has two entrances; both work well but you'll see different things on the way in, depending on which one you use.

The **west entrance** (where this tour begins) is near Mars Hill (to the right as you face the Acropolis from the Plaka). From the Plaka, fix your eyes on the Acropolis, start walking uphill veering right, and find the roads that funnel you there. To reach the west entrance from south of the Acropolis, head up the path that splits off from Dionysiou Areopagitou street.

The **south entrance,** at the base of the Acropolis and next to the Acropolis Museum, is often less crowded (Metro: Akropoli). You'll climb a steep-but-shady tree-lined path and pick up our tour at the first stop (you can see the Theater of Dionysus—described near the end of this chapter—on the way up, and Mars Hill—listed in the Sights chapter—at the end).

Note that there's no way to reach the Acropolis without a lot of climbing (though wheelchair users can take an elevator—from the west ticket booth, go around the left side of the hilltop).

Figure a 10- to 20-minute hike from the base of the Acropolis up to the hilltop archaeological site.

Visitor Information: Supplement the tour in this chapter with the free information brochure (you may have to ask for it when you buy your ticket) and info plaques posted throughout.

Tours: Consider making advance arrangements with one of my recommended local guides (see the Activities chapter). Avoid the guides at the entrance who tend to be rude, overpriced, and underqualified.

🎧 Download my free Acropolis **audio tour.** This sight is particularly suited to an audio tour, as it allows your eyes to enjoy the wonders of the Acropolis while your ears learn its story.

Length of This Tour: Allow two hours.

Baggage Check: Backpacks are allowed; baby strollers are not. There's a checkroom just below the west ticket booth near Mars Hill.

Services: There are WCs at the Acropolis ticket booths and more WCs and drinking fountains atop the Acropolis in the former museum building (behind the Parthenon). Picnicking is not allowed on the premises. Near the west ticket booth are a drinking fountain, machines selling cheap bottles of cold water, and a juice/snack stand. Flanking the south entrance are cafés, shops, and newsstands selling food, water, and souvenirs; the Athens TI is also nearby, with good information and free WCs.

Plan Ahead: Wear sensible shoes—Acropolis paths are steep and uneven. In summer, it gets very hot on top, so take a hat, sunscreen, sunglasses, and a bottle of water.

Starring: The Parthenon and other monuments from the Golden Age, plus great views of Athens and beyond.

Acropolis Overview

STANDING RUINS
ORIGINAL FOOTPRINT

To Ancient Agora

To Monastiraki

ANAFIOTIKA

Mars Hill

THEORIAS

ELEVATOR

ERECHTHEION

To Plaka

ACROPOLIS FLAG

PROPYLAEA

BEULÉ GATE

STRATONOS

To Plaka

TICKETS & WC

THESPIDOS

TEMPLE OF ATHENA NIKE

PARTHENON

WC

EPIMENIDOU

WEST ENTRANCE

THEASSILOU

ODEON OF HERODES ATTICUS

To Apostolou Pavlou & Thissio

DIONYSIOU AREOPAGITOU

THEATER OF DIONYSUS

& WC

GARIVALDI

PROPYLEON

ERECTHIOU

PARTHENONOS

SOUTH ENTRANCE

BUS PARKING LOT

Filopappos Hill

ROVERTOU GALLI

MAKRIGIANNI

KALLISPERI

Akropoli

100 Meters

100 Yards

ACROPOLIS MUSEUM

Akropoli M

BACKGROUND

The Acropolis has been the heart of Athens since the beginning of recorded time. This limestone plateau, faced with sheer, 100-foot cliffs and fed by permanent springs, was a natural fortress. The Mycenaeans (c. 1400 BC) ruled the area from their palace on this hilltop, and Athena—the patron goddess of the city—was worshipped here from around 800 BC on.

But everything changed in 480 BC when Persia invaded Greece for the second time. As the Persians approached, the Athenians evacuated the city, abandoning it to be looted and vandalized. All the temples atop the Acropolis were burned to the ground. The Athenians fought back at sea, winning an improbable naval victory at the Battle of Salamis. The Persians were driven out of Greece, and Athens found

The Acropolis' sheer cliffs have made it a natural fortress since the beginning of time.

itself suddenly victorious. Cash poured into Athens from the other Greek city-states, which were eager to be allied with the winning side.

By 450 BC, Athens was at the peak of its power and the treasury was flush with money...but in the city center, the Acropolis still lay empty, a vast blank canvas. Athens' leader at the time, Pericles, was ambitious and farsighted. He funneled Athens' newfound wealth into a massive rebuilding program. Led by the visionary architect/sculptor Pheidias (490-430 BC), the Athenians transformed the Acropolis into a complex of supersized, ornate temples worthy of the city's protector, Athena.

The Parthenon, Erechtheion, Propylaea, and Temple of Athena Nike were built as a coherent ensemble (c. 450-400 BC). Unlike most ancient sites, which have layer upon layer of ruins from different periods, the Acropolis we see today was started and finished within two generations—a snapshot of the Golden Age set in stone.

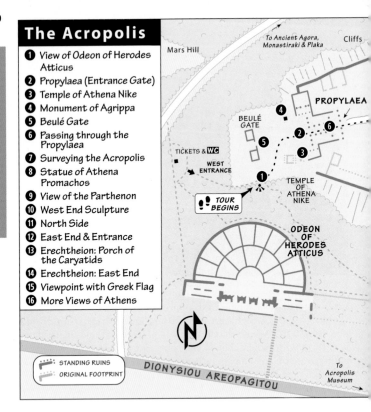

The Acropolis

1 View of Odeon of Herodes Atticus
2 Propylaea (Entrance Gate)
3 Temple of Athena Nike
4 Monument of Agrippa
5 Beulé Gate
6 Passing through the Propylaea
7 Surveying the Acropolis
8 Statue of Athena Promachos
9 View of the Parthenon
10 West End Sculpture
11 North Side
12 East End & Entrance
13 Erechtheion: Porch of the Caryatids
14 Erechtheion: East End
15 Viewpoint with Greek Flag
16 More Views of Athens

Mars Hill

To Ancient Agora, Monastiraki & Plaka · Cliffs

PROPYLAEA

BEULÉ GATE

TICKETS & WC

WEST ENTRANCE

TOUR BEGINS

TEMPLE OF ATHENA NIKE

ODEON OF HERODES ATTICUS

STANDING RUINS
ORIGINAL FOOTPRINT

DIONYSIOU AREOPAGITOU

To Acropolis Museum

THE TOUR BEGINS

▶ Our route starts at the **west entrance,** near Mars Hill. (If you enter via the south entrance, just follow the path up, where you'll join our tour at the first stop—you can see Mars Hill after the visit.)

Before entering, check out the huge, craggy boulder of **Mars Hill** (a.k.a. Areopagus), just downhill (toward the Agora) from the ticket booth. Consider climbing this rock for great views of the Acropolis' ancient entry gate, the Propylaea, and the Ancient Agora. Mars Hill's

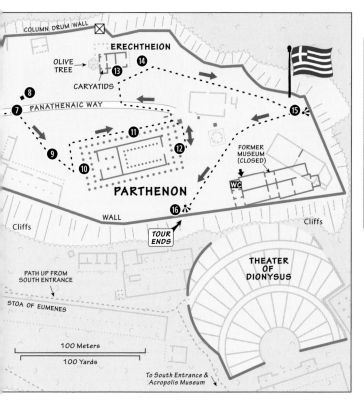

bare, polished rock is extremely slippery—a metal staircase to the left helps somewhat. (For more on Mars Hill and its role in Christian history, see page 135.)

Before you show your ticket and enter the Acropolis site, make sure you have everything you'll need for your visit. Once inside, there are no services except WCs and water fountains.

▶ *Enter the site and start climbing the paths that wind up the hill, following signs on this one-way tourist route (bearing to the right). Before you reach the summit, peel off to the right for a...*

Odeon theater, for ancients and moderns   Propylaea entrance, as seen from Mars Hill

❶ View of the Odeon of Herodes Atticus

This large 5,000-seat amphitheater built during the Roman era is still used today for performances. From this perch you get a good look at the stage setup. The three-quarter-circle floor was the stage. There, musicians and actors performed in the Greek style. Rising behind it are the overgrown remnants of a raised stage and a stage wall for the backdrop (which were not used in traditional Greek theater but were common for Roman-style spectacles). Originally, the theater had a wood-and-tile roof as well.

The *odeon* was built in 161 AD by Herodes Atticus, a wealthy landowner, in memory of his wife. Herodes was a Greek with Roman citizenship. He was a legendary orator and a friend of Emperor Hadrian. This amphitheater is the most famous of the many impressive buildings Herodes financed around the country. Greeks know it's technically an *odeon,* namely a theater used mainly for songs ("odes") rather than drama.

In the 1950s, the ruined theater was reconstructed. Now on many summer nights it hosts music, dance, and theatrical performances under the stars.

▶ *Back on the path, bear left and continue uphill to the grand entrance gate of the Acropolis: the Propylaea. Stand at the foot of the (very) steep marble staircase, facing up toward the big Doric columns.*

As you face the Propylaea, to your left is a tall, grayish stone pedestal with nothing on it: the Monument of Agrippa. On your right, atop the wall, is the Temple of Athena Nike. Behind you stands a doorway in a wall, known as the Beulé Gate.

❷ Propylaea

The entrance to the Acropolis couldn't be through just any old gate; it had to be the grandest gate ever built. Ancient visitors would stand here, catching their breath before the final push to the summit, and admire these gleaming columns and steep steps that almost fill your field of vision. Imagine the psychological impact this awe-inspiring, colonnaded entryway to the sacred rock must have had on ancient Athenians.

The Propylaea (pro-PEE-leh-ah) is U-shaped, with a large central hallway (the six Doric columns), flanked by side wings that reach out to embrace the visitor. The central building looked like a mini Parthenon, with Doric columns topped by a triangular pediment. Originally, the Propylaea was painted bright colors.

The left wing of the Propylaea was the Pinakotheke, or "painting gallery." In ancient times this space contained artwork and housed visiting dignitaries and VIPs.

The buildings of the Acropolis were all constructed within about a 50-year span, and they were intended to complement one another. The Propylaea was built in five short years (437-432 BC, by Mnesicles). Both buildings are Doric (with Ionic touches) and are aligned east-west, with columns of similar width-to-height ratios. In other words, the Propylaea welcomed the visitor with an appropriately grand first taste of the Acropolis they were about to enter.

▸ *Before ascending, notice the monuments flanking the entryway. To the right of the Propylaea, look up high atop the block wall to find the…*

Climbing the Propylaea's staircase

Temple of Nike, overlooking the Propylaea

❸ Temple of Athena Nike

This little temple—nearly square, 11 feet tall, with four columns at both ends—had delightful proportions. Where the Parthenon and Propylaea are sturdy Doric, this temple pioneered the Ionic style in Athens, with elegant scroll-topped columns. The Temple of Athena Nike (NEEK-ee) was started a few years after the Propylaea was finished (c. 427-421/415 BC). It was designed by Callicrates, one of the architects of the Parthenon.

The Acropolis was mainly dedicated to the goddess Athena, patron of the city. At this temple, she was worshiped for bringing the Athenians victory ("Nike"). A statue of Athena inside the temple celebrated the turning-point victory over the Persians at the Battle of Plataea in 479 BC. It was also meant to help ensure future victory over the Spartans in the ongoing Peloponnesian War. The statue was never given wings because Athenians wanted Athena to stay and protect their city—hence the place became known as the Temple of Wingless Athena.

▶ *To the left (as you face the Propylaea) is a gray-stone pedestal, the...*

❹ Monument of Agrippa

The pedestal—even without anything on it—reaches as high as the Temple of Athena Nike. It's 25 feet tall, made of gray marble with yellow veins. Several statues have graced this prime location. Originally, it held a bronze statue of a four-horse chariot. The driver was the race champion at the Olympic Games held in 178 BC.

Over the centuries, this pedestal has supported many egos. Each ruler of Athens wanted to put his mark on the mighty Acropolis. When Rome occupied the city, Marc Antony placed a statue of himself and his girlfriend Cleopatra atop the pedestal. After their defeat, the Roman general Agrippa (son-in-law of Augustus) replaced it with a statue of himself (in 27 BC).

It was the Romans who expanded the Propylaea, by building the structure at the base of the stairs—the ❺ **Beulé Gate.** This ceremonial doorway became the official entrance to the Acropolis, making the Propylaea entry even grander.

▶ *Climb the steps (or today's switchback ramps for visitors). Partway up, try to pull off to one side—out of the steady tourist torrent—to take a closer look inside the Propylaea.*

The Monument of Agrippa once held grand statues of Athens' heroes and rulers.

Roman-built Beulé Gate

Stackable column drum, in the Propylaea

❻ Passing Through the Propylaea

Imagine being part of the grand parade of the Great Panathenaic Festival, held every four years. The procession started a mile away, at Athens' city gate, passed through the Agora, up past Mars Hill, and through the Propylaea. Men on horseback, musicians, dignitaries, and maidens carrying gifts for the gods all ascended these stairs. In those days, there was a ramp in the middle of the staircase, which narrowed as they ascended, funneling them into the central passageway. There were five doorways into the Propylaea, one between each of the six columns.

The Propylaea passageway had a roof. The marble-tile ceiling, now partially restored, was painted sky blue and studded with stars. Floral designs decorated other parts of the building. The interior columns are Ionic, a bit thinner than the Doric columns of the exterior. You'll pass by some big column drums with square holes in the center, where iron pins once held the drums in place. Greek columns were not usually made from a single piece of stone, but from sections—"column drums"—stacked on top of one another.

▶ *The Propylaea and its monuments are certainly impressive. But this is just the opening act. Pass through the Propylaea. As you emerge out the other end, you're on top of the Acropolis. There it is—the Parthenon! Just like in the books (except for the scaffolding). Pause and take it all in.*

❼ Surveying the Acropolis

The "Acropolis rock" is a mostly flat limestone ridge covering seven acres, scattered with ruins. There's the Parthenon ahead to the right. To the left of that, with the six lady-columns (Caryatids), is the

Erechtheion. The Panathenaic Way ran between them. The processional street and the buildings were aligned east–west, like the hill.

Ancient visitors standing here would have come face-to-face with an imposing statue of Athena, 30 feet tall, carrying a shield and a spear. This **❽ statue of Athena Promachos** once stood between the Propylaea and the Erechtheion. Today there's just a field of rubble, with the statue's former location marked by three stones forming a low wall.

The Athena Promachos was one of three well-known statues of Athena on the Acropolis. As the patron goddess of the city, Athena was worshipped for her wisdom, her purity, and her strength. Here she appeared in "strength" mode, as a "Frontline Soldier" (*promachos*), armed and ready for battle. The bronze statue was cast by Pheidias, the man in charge of the overall design of the Acropolis. It was so tall that the shining tip of Athena's spear was visible from ships at sea, 30 miles away. The statue disappeared in ancient times, and no one knows its fate.

▸ *Move a little closer for the classic view of the world's most famous*

For 2,000 years, the Parthenon's west end has greeted visitors.

temple. If you're tired, I've installed a handy white marble bench for you to take a load off while you take in the...

❾ View of the Parthenon

The Parthenon is the hill's showstopper—the finest temple in the ancient world, standing on the highest point of the Acropolis, 490 feet above sea level. The Parthenon is now largely in ruins, partly from the ravages of time, but mostly from a freak accident in 1687 (see the "After the Golden Age" sidebar, later).

Imagine how awesome the Parthenon must have looked when it was completed nearly 2,500 years ago. It's the largest Doric temple in Greece—228 feet long and 101 feet wide. Its footprint covers more than 23,000 square feet.

At each end were eight fluted **Doric columns.** Along each side were 17 columns, for a total of 46. In addition, there were 19 inner columns in the Ionic style. The outer columns are 34 feet high and 6 feet in diameter. In its heyday, the temple was decorated with statues and carved reliefs, all painted in vivid colors. It's considered Greece's greatest Doric temple (though not its purest textbook example because it incorporates Ionic columns and sculpture).

The Parthenon served the cult of Athena the Virgin, with a statue of the goddess inside. It also served as the Fort Knox-like treasury of Athens. The west end is the classic view that greets visitors—but the building's main entrance was at the other end.

This awe-inspiring temple was completed in less than a decade—from around 450 to 440 BC. The sculptural decoration took a few more years. The project's overall "look" was supervised by the master sculptor-architect Pheidias. The construction was handled by

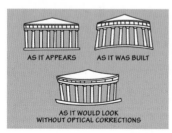

AS IT APPEARS   AS IT WAS BUILT

AS IT WOULD LOOK
WITHOUT OPTICAL CORRECTIONS

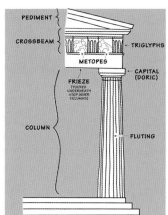

well-known architects Ictinus and Callicrates. The two main sculptors were Agoracritos and Alcamenes.

It's big, sure. But what makes the Parthenon truly exceptional is that the architects used a whole bagful of **optical illusions** to give the building an ever-so-subtle feeling of balance, strength, and harmonious beauty.

For example, look at the temple's steps. Architects know that a long, flat baseline on a building looks to the human eye like it's sagging, and that parallel columns appear to bend away from each other. To create a building that looked harmonious, the Parthenon's ancient architects compensated. The base of the Parthenon actually arches several inches upward in the middle to counteract the "sagging" illusion.

Now check out the columns. They tilt ever so slightly inward (one of the reasons why the Parthenon has withstood earthquakes so well). If you extended the columns upward several miles, they'd eventually touch. Also, the corner columns are thicker than the rest to make them appear the same size. And all of the columns bulge imperceptibly halfway up, giving the subconscious impression of stout, barrel-chested men bearing the weight of the roof. For a building that seems at first to be all about right angles, the Parthenon is amazingly short on straight lines.

All these clever refinements form a powerful subconscious impression on the viewer that brings an otherwise boring architectural box to life. It's amazing to think that all this was planned and implemented in stone so long ago.

❿ West End Sculpture

The statues and carved reliefs that once decorated the Parthenon are now mostly eroded or missing. The cream of the crop are in the British Museum in London and are called the Elgin Marbles. (For details, see the "After the Golden Age" sidebar, later.) A few pieces are in Athens' Acropolis Museum.

But try to imagine this grand temple in its prime. Originally, the Parthenon's sculptures were all painted in bright colors, and the building looked much livelier than today's stately gray ruin. Look up at the crossbeam atop the eight columns, decorated with panels of relief carvings called **metopes.** These depict Athenians battling that legendary race of female warriors, the Amazons. Originally there were 92 Doric-style metopes in high relief, mostly designed by Pheidias himself.

The crossbeams once supported a triangular pediment (now gone). This area was once filled in with statues, showing Athena with her olive tree competing with Poseidon and his trident to be Athens' patron god. Today just one statue remains (and it's a reconstruction).

Move closer and look between the eight columns. Inside, there's another row of eight columns, supporting a covered entrance porch. Look up above the inner columns. Decorating those crossbeams are

Metope—carved relief on the crossbeam

Pediment statues depict Athena's triumph.

more relief carvings—the "frieze." Originally, a 525-foot-long **frieze** of panels circled the entire building. It showed the Panathenaic parade—women, men on horseback, musicians, sacrificial animals being led to the slaughter—while the gods looked on.

If you're having trouble envisioning all this, you can see many of these sculptures in the flesh at the Acropolis Museum, at the base of the hill. The museum was built to house Greece's collection...and to try to entice the rest back from museums around the world.

▶ *Continue along the long left (north) side of the Parthenon.*

⓫ North Side

This view of the Parthenon gives you a glimpse into how the temple was constructed.

Look between the columns—you can see remnants of the interior walls. These were built with thousands of rectangular blocks. The temple interior consisted of an entry hall and a *cella*. The *cella* was the inner sanctum, where Athena was worshipped. The roof was made of wooden beams—now long gone. The roof tiles were made of ultra-white, translucent marble from the island of Paros, so the interior actually glowed.

Now concentrate on the columns that surround the Parthenon. These formed an open-air porch around the inner sanctum. The columns are in the Doric style—stout, lightly fluted, with no base. The capitals on top of the columns are simple, consisting of a plate topped with a square slab. The capitals alone weigh 12 tons.

The Parthenon's builders used only the very finest materials. The white Pentelic marble came from Mount Pentelikon, 10 miles away. Unlike the grand structures of the Egyptians (pyramids) and the Romans (Colosseum), the Parthenon was built not by slaves but by free men who drew a salary (though it's possible that slaves worked at the quarries).

The Parthenon was constructed from 100,000 tons of marble. Imagine the engineering problems of quarrying and transporting all that stone. Most likely the **column drums** (5-10 tons each) were cut at the quarry and rolled here. To hoist the drums in place, the builders used four-poster cranes (and Greek mathematics), centering the drums with a cedar peg in the middle. The drums were held together by metal pins that were coated in lead to prevent corrosion, then fitted into a square hole cut in the center of the drum.

Remember that the Parthenon is intentionally off-kilter in places for aesthetic effect. Each piece was sized and cut for a specific location. The Parthenon's stones are so well-crafted that they fit together within a fraction of an inch. The total cost to build the Parthenon (in today's money) has been estimated at over a billion dollars.

▸ *If you see cranes and scaffolding here, it's part of a heroic effort to shore the structure up against the ravages of pollution. Continue on to the...*

⑫ East End and Entrance

This end was the original entrance to the temple. Over the doorway, the triangular pediment depicted the central event in Athenian history—the **birth of Athena,** their patron goddess. Today, the pediment barely survives, and the original statues of the gods are partly in the British Museum. Originally, the gods were gathered at a banquet (see a copy of the reclining Dionysus at the far left—looking so drunk he's afraid to come down). Zeus got a headache and asked Hephaistos to

Devotees once entered at the east end.

relieve it. As the other gods looked on in astonishment, Hephaistos split Zeus' head open, and—at the peak of the pediment—out rose Athena. The now-missing statues were surprisingly realistic and three-dimensional, with perfect anatomy and bulging muscles showing through transparent robes.

Imagine this spot during the age of Pericles and Socrates, on the big day—the **Panathenaic Festival:**

The Parthenon is gleaming white, adorned with painted statues. It sits on a grassy field. The parade gathers here at the entrance. Musicians play flutes, girls dance, and riders rein in their restless steeds. On open-air altars, the priests make an offering to Athena—100 oxen, the ultimate sacrificial gift to the gods.

A select few are allowed to go inside. They proceed up the steps, through the majestic columns, and into the *cella*. It's cavernous—100 feet long, 60 feet wide, and four stories tall, with a pool in the middle. At the far end of the room towers an enormous 40-foot tall statue of **Athena Parthenos** (Athena the Virgin), wearing a soldier's helmet, with a shield by her side. Athena's left hand holds a spear. Her other hand has a small statue of Nike—she literally holds Victory in the palm of her hand.

The statue was the work of the master Pheidias himself (c. 440 BC). It was made of wood, plated with ivory for skin, and a ton of gold for her garments. It stood here for 800 years, until it was carried off to Constantinople, where it subsequently vanished.

During the Panathenaic parade, the citizens of Athens would approach the statue of Athena and present the goddess with a newly woven robe. In return, Athena would ensure the continuing success of the great city of Athens.

▶ *Our next stop is the Erechtheion, the temple across the street. (But perhaps most important right now is the modern brown-brick building nearby, with WCs and a drinking fountain.)*

Approach the Erechtheion. Start by enjoying the porch supported by six statues.

⑬ Erechtheion: Porch of the Caryatids

Though overshadowed by the more impressive Parthenon, the Erechtheion was perhaps more prestigious. It stood on one of the oldest sites on the hill, where the Mycenaeans had built their palace centuries before. (Those huge ruined stones scattered in front of the Erechtheion are all that's left of the Mycenaean palace.)

The temple's most famous feature is the **Porch of the Caryatids.** An inspired piece of architecture, this balcony has six beautiful maidens functioning as columns that support the roof. Each of the **lady-columns** has a base beneath her feet, pleated robes as the fluting, a fruit-basket hat as the capital, and—in the back—locks of hair as buttresses. Both feminine and functional, they pose gracefully, exposing a hint of leg. The Caryatids were modeled on and named after the women of Karyai, near Sparta, famous for their upright posture and noble character. (These are faithful copies of the originals. Five of the originals are on display in the Acropolis Museum).

Near the porch—below and to the left—notice the **olive tree.** Greece has 140 million of these trees. Though this particular tree is not ancient, there's been an olive tree on this spot for thousands of years. It marks the sacred place where, according to legend, Athena first planted one. Olive trees have been called "the gift of Athena to Athens."

▶ *Let's view the Erechtheion from a different angle. Walk to the right, to the east end of the structure. Find a spot where you can look through the six columns and get a sense of what the temple was like inside.*

⓮ Erechtheion: East End

This unique, two-story temple fits nicely into the slope of the hill. The east end (with the six Ionic columns) was the upper-level entrance. The lower entrance was on the north side (to your right, 10 feet lower), where you can see six more Ionic columns. By the way, it's those columns that are the "face of the Acropolis" that Athenians see from the Plaka below.

The Erechtheion was constructed around 410 BC. The architect, Mnesicles, was the same man who did the Propylaea. Whereas the Propylaea and the Parthenon are both sturdy Doric style, the Erechtheion is elegant Ionic. The columns are thinner, more deeply fluted, and topped with a scroll-like capital. In its day, the Erechtheion was a stunning building of white Pentelic marble, with black trim and painted columns.

Now look inside the temple. You can make out that the inner worship hall, the *cella,* is divided in two by walls (more on that in a minute).

Erechtheion's Caryatids—these stone maidens support the roof of this prestigious temple.

The Erechtheion sits atop temple ruins.   Greece's flag flies proudly above the city.

The Erechtheion also once held a life-size statue of Athena made of olive wood depicting her as **Athena Polias,** Protector of the City. Dating from about 900 BC, this statue was much older and more venerable than either of Pheidias' colossal statues. It supposedly dropped from the sky as a gift from Athena herself. It was so revered that, when the Persians invaded, Pericles took the statue for safekeeping as the Athenians evacuated their city.

The Erechtheion is supposedly the spot where Athena and Poseidon fought it out for naming rights to the city. Poseidon threw his trident, which opened a gash in the earth to bring forth the gift of water. It left a diagonal crack still visible in the pavement of the lower, north entrance. (Cynics say it was lightning.) Athena won the contest by stabbing a rock with her spear. This sprouted the blessed olive tree that stood near the Porch of the Caryatids. The twin *cellas* of the Erechtheion allowed the worship of both gods—Athena and Poseidon. They're side by side, to show that they were still friends.

▶ *Look to the right (beyond the Plaka-facing porch). The modern **elevator** carries people with limited mobility up to the Acropolis. The north wall of the Acropolis has a retaining wall built from **column drums** from remains of a half-finished temple destroyed when Persia invaded in 480 BC. The Athenians rebuilt as fast as they could with the scattered material to fortify the city against Sparta.*

Turn 180 degrees and walk to the far end of the Acropolis. There you'll find an observation platform with a giant Greek flag.

⓯ Viewpoint with Greek Flag

The Greek flag's blue-and-white stripes symbolize the nine syllables of the Greek phrase for "Freedom or Death." That phrase took on new meaning when the Nazis entered Athens in April 1941. According to an oft-repeated (but unverified) story, the Nazis confronted a Greek soldier who was guarding this flag, and ordered him to remove it. He calmly took it down, wrapped himself in it—and jumped to his death. A month later, two heroic teenagers, Manolis Glezos and Apostolis Santas, scaled the wall, took down the Nazi flag and raised the Greek flag. This was one of the first well-known acts of resistance against the Nazis, and the boys' bravery is honored by a plaque near the base of the steps. To this day, Greeks can see this flag from just about any-where in Athens and think of their hard-won independence.

From this observation deck, you have a great **view of Athens.** The Ancient Agora spreads below the Acropolis, and the sprawl of modern Athens whitewashes the surrounding hills. In 1830, the population of Athens' core was about 5,000. By 1900, it was 600,000, and during the 1920s, with the influx of Greeks from Turkey, the population surged to 1.5 million. The city's expansion could barely keep up with its explod-ing population. With the boom times in the 1950s and 1980s, the city grew to nearly four million. Pan around. From this perch you're look-ing at the homes of one out of every three Greeks.

Looking down on the **Plaka,** find (looking left to right) the Ancient Agora, with its Temple of Hephaistos. Next comes the Roman Forum (the four columns and palm trees) with its round, white, domed Temple of the Winds monument. The **Anafiotika** neighborhood clings to the Acropolis hillside directly below us. About eight blocks beyond that, find the dome of the cathedral.

Farther in the distance, **Lykavittos Hill,** Athens' highest point, is crowned with the Chapel of St. George (and an expensive view restau-rant; cable car up the hill). Looking still farther in the distance, you'll see lighter-colored bits on the mountains behind—these are **Pentelic quarries,** the source of the marble used to build (and now restore) the monuments of the Acropolis.

As you continue panning to the right, you'll spot the beige Neoclassical **Parliament** building, marking Syntagma Square; the **National Garden** is behind and to the right of it. In the garden is the yellow **Zappeion,** an exhibition hall. The green area in the far dis-tance contains the 60,000-seat, marble **Panathenaic Stadium**—an ancient venue (on the site where Golden Age Athens held its games), which was rehabbed in 1896 to help revive the modern Olympics.

After the Golden Age: The Acropolis Through History

Classical: The Parthenon and the rest of the Acropolis buildings survived through classical times largely intact, despite Herulian looting (AD 267). As the Roman Empire declined, precious items were carried off, including the 40-foot Athena statue from the Parthenon.

Christian: After nearly a thousand years as Athena's temple, the Parthenon became a Christian church (fifth century AD). Pagan sculptures and decorations were removed (or renamed), and the interior was decorated with colorful Christian frescoes. The west end of the building became the main entrance, and the interior was reconfigured with an apse at the east end.

Muslim: In 1456, the Turks arrived and converted the Parthenon into a mosque, adding a minaret. The Propylaea gateway was used as a palace for the Turkish ruler of Athens. The Turks also used the Parthenon to store gunpowder, unfortunately leading to the greatest catastrophe in the Acropolis' long history. It happened in...

1687: A Venetian army laid siege to the Acropolis. The Venetians didn't

▶ *Complete your visual tour of Athens at the south edge of the Acropolis. To reach the viewpoint, walk back toward the Parthenon, going past it to the left to the cliff-top wall.*

⑯ More Views of Athens

Look to the left. In the near distance are the huge columns of the **Temple of Olympian Zeus.** Begun in the sixth century BC, it wasn't finished until the time of the Roman emperor Hadrian, 700 years later. It was the biggest temple in all of Greece, with 104 Corinthian pillars housing a 40-foot seated statue of Zeus, a replica of the famous one created by Pheidias in Olympia. This area was part of Hadrian's

care about ancient architecture. As far as they were concerned, it was a lucky hit of mortar fire that triggered the massive explosion that ripped the center out of the Parthenon, rattled the Propylaea and the other buildings, and wiped out the Turkish defenders.

Lord Elgin: In 1801, Lord Elgin, the British ambassador to the Ottomans in Constantinople, got "permission" from the sultan to gather

sculptures from the Parthenon, buy them from locals, and even saw them off the building. He carted half of them to London. Although a few original frieze, metope, and pediment carvings still adorn the Parthenon, most of the sculptures are on display in museums, including the nearby Acropolis Museum.

From Independence to the Present: In the 19th century, newly independent Greece tore down the Parthenon's minaret and the other post-Classical buildings atop the Acropolis, turning it into an archaeological zone. Since then the site has been excavated and has undergone several renovations.

"new Athens," a planned community in his day, complete with the triumphal **Arch of Hadrian** near the temple.

The **Theater of Dionysus,** with its illustrious history, lies in ruins at your feet. It's fair to say that this is where our culture's great tradition of theater was born. During Athens' Golden Age, Sophocles and others watched their plays performed here. Originally just grass with a circular dirt area as the stage, the theater was eventually expanded, and stone seating added, to accommodate 17,000 patrons in about 330 BC, during the time of Alexander the Great. During Roman times, a raised stage was added, and the theater was connected to the Odeon of Herodes Atticus by a long, covered stoa, creating an ensemble of inviting venues. Today, plans are afoot to restore the theater to its former

View of Lykavittos Hill

South view of the Temple of Olympian Zeus

greatness. It's free to visit the theater with your Acropolis ticket (it's only accessible from inside the Acropolis site—see the end of the tour for directions).

Beyond the theater is the wonderful **Acropolis Museum,** a black-and-gray modern glass building, with three rectangular floors stacked at irregular angles atop each other. The top floor, which houses replicas and some originals of the Parthenon's art, is angled to match the orientation of that great temple.

Looking right, you see **Filopappos Hill**—the green, tree-dotted hill topped with a marble funerary monument to a popular Roman senator, Philopappos, who died in the early second century. This hill is where the Venetians launched the infamous mortar attack of 1687 that destroyed the Parthenon. Today, a theater here hosts popular folk-dancing performances (described in the Activities chapter).

Farther in the distance, you get a glimpse of the turquoise waters of the **Aegean** (the only island visible is Aegina). While the Persians were burning the Acropolis to the ground, the Athenians watched from their ships as they prepared to defeat their foes in the history-changing Battle of Salamis. In the distance, far to the right, is the port of Piraeus. Today Piraeus is the main departure point for boats to the islands, but it's also the ancient port from which Athenian ships sailed and returned with the wealth that made this city so great.

▶ *Our tour is finished. Enjoy a few final moments with the Acropolis before you leave.*

The Acropolis exits are back the way you came—through the Propylaea. From here, you can exit either on the west side (go through the Beulé Gate) or to the south (go back toward the Odeon of Herodes Atticus, turn left, and walk downhill along the path).

The ruins of the Theater of Dionysus, which once staged works by Sophocles

Exit from the west side if you want to visit Mars Hill on the way out. Or passing Mars Hill, you can head to the Plaka and Ancient Agora (follow the roads winding downhill), or the Acropolis Museum (turn left on the pedestrian boulevard, walk down to Dionysiou Areopagitou street, and turn left).

To reach the Theater of Dionysus, head toward the south entrance. From there, consider visiting the Acropolis Museum, which is across the street from the south entrance.

Acropolis Museum Tour

Μουσείο Ακρόπολης

Athens' Acropolis Museum is a custom-built showcase for sculptures from the Acropolis, starring its greatest temple, the Parthenon.

This tour starts with broken fragments from the Acropolis' earliest temples, then focuses on the great works of the Acropolis' glory years—roughly 500-400 BC—before ascending to the top floor for the museum's star attraction: the Parthenon's sculptures laid out in the exact dimensions of the Parthenon itself.

The museum works equally well either before you visit the Acropolis or afterward. There's a convenient entrance/exit that connects the two sights. With its striking exterior and irreplaceable Acropolis statues, the Acropolis Museum is the boldest symbol yet of today's Athens.

ORIENTATION

Cost: €10.

Hours: Daily 8:00-20:00 except Mon until 16:00, Fri until 22:00; Nov-March Mon-Thu 9:00-17:00, Fri until 22:00, Sat-Sun until 20:00.

Information: Tel. 210-900-0900, www.theacropolismuseum.gr.

Getting There: It's the giant modern building facing the south side of the Acropolis from across the broad Dionysiou Areopagitou pedestrian drag. The museum is next to the Akropoli Metro stop on Makrigianni, a street lined with restaurants.

Visitor Information: Pick up a free map at the information desk. Museum guards (with red badges) can answer questions, and a 13-minute video plays continuously in the upper atrium (level 3).

Baggage Check: There's a free bag check at the counter near the turnstiles at the base of the ramp (required for big bags). If you're dining at the museum's restaurant after your visit, note that the bag check closes when the museum does.

Length of This Tour: Allow 1.5 hours.

Services: A gift shop and a café are on the ground floor; level 2 has a bookstore and a pricey restaurant with smashing views.

Starring: Marble masterpieces from one of the most influential archaeological sites in human history—and high hopes that more will eventually join the collection.

THE TOUR BEGINS

The eye-catching, glassy building—designed by Swiss-born, New York-based architect Bernard Tschumi—gives a postmodern jolt to Athens' concrete cityscape. Its lower level is aligned with ancient foundations beneath it, while the top floor sits askew, mirroring the nearby Parthenon. The glass walls allow visitors to enjoy the artifacts inside while gazing out at the Acropolis itself.

Be aware that many statues here—though original and very historic—are pretty ruined and less impressive than, say, the Parthenon sculptures ("Elgin Marbles") in London's British Museum. But the Acropolis Museum more than makes up for that with high-quality copies, its Parthenon-replica layout, and nifty modern displays that bring the ruins to life. The museum is a sort of 21st-century Trojan horse, intended to lure the "Elgin Marbles" back to Athens. For years, the Brits have claimed that Greece can't give those ancient treasures a suitable home. But now Athens can proudly say, "Oh really?"

▶ *Enter on the ground floor (level 0) and buy your ticket.*

Level 0

Browse a few introductory displays (about the Acropolis' evolution from 1200 BC to AD 1500), then go through the turnstiles onto a wide ramp.

❶ The Ramp

Look through the ramp's glass floor at the ancient ruins excavated beneath the museum. These were houses and shops of a once-lively neighborhood here at the base of the Acropolis (the excavation is included with your ticket and is worth a quick look at the end of your visit—look for an access ramp at the museum entrance). As no one actually lived on top of the Acropolis, which was reserved for the temples of the gods, ancient Athenians either settled down here or over by the

Agora. The artifacts you see here, found on the hill's slopes, symbolize the transition from the everyday world below to the sacred realm above.

Case #5 (on the left), with ancient vases painted with wedding scenes, makes it clear that the Acropolis was a popular place to get married.

As Athenians ascended the hill to worship the gods, they brought offerings (like the vases and figurines in **Case #6,** on the left) to bribe the gods to answer their prayers.

They might stop at the **Sanctuary of Dionysus** (described in another display on the left), which had a theater built into the slope of the Acropolis just uphill from today's museum. Devotees of Dionysus would drink wine while watching performers sing ecstatic songs or recite poems.

Just before the stairs, on the right, find the square stone **treasure box** (offering box), where worshippers of Aphrodite would drop in a silver drachma to ensure a good love life.

▶ *Let's ascend to the sacred realm of the gods. Climb the stairs at the end of the ramp. Straight ahead is a collection of statues in a triangular frame.*

Level 1

This floor has statues from the Acropolis' first temples, a century before the Parthenon.

❷ Pediment of the Hekatompedon

This triangular-shaped set of statues adorned the entrance to the first great temple on the Acropolis (from 570 BC). It was called the Hekatompedon ("100-foot-long") for its legendary size. The temple was dedicated to Athena, the patron of the city of Athens, and it stood in the Acropolis' prime location—right where the Parthenon is today.

On the left, bearded Hercules wrestles with the dragon-tailed sea monster Triton. In the (very damaged) center, two lions kill a bull. To the right is a three-headed demon with a snake tail. These dapper, bearded gentle-demons hold objects representing the elements of wind, water, and fire—perhaps symbolizing the struggle of man versus nature. On display nearby (behind and to the right) is another Hekatompedon statue—a mama lion feasting on a bull.

Acropolis Museum—Level 1

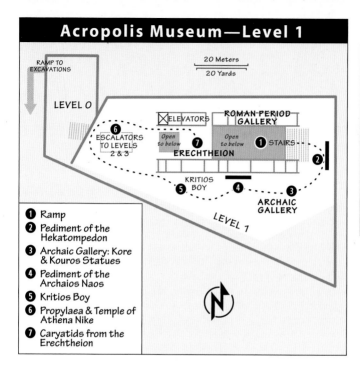

RAMP TO EXCAVATIONS

LEVEL O

20 Meters
20 Yards

ELEVATORS

ROMAN-PERIOD GALLERY

6 ESCALATORS TO LEVELS 2 & 3

Open to below

7

Open to below

1 STAIRS

ERECHTHEION

2

KRITIOS BOY

5

4

3

ARCHAIC GALLERY

LEVEL 1

1 Ramp
2 Pediment of the Hekatompedon
3 Archaic Gallery: Kore & Kouros Statues
4 Pediment of the Archaios Naos
5 Kritios Boy
6 Propylaea & Temple of Athena Nike
7 Caryatids from the Erechtheion

▶ Let's see more non-Parthenon statues. Turn right (past the feasting lion) and enter a gallery flooded with daylight and columns spanning the room.

❸ Archaic Gallery: Kore and Kouros Statues

These statues were gifts to the gods, to decorate the gods' homes atop the Acropolis—that is, their temples.

The **horses and riders** were likely donated by rich benefactors to thank the gods for letting them win the local horse races. The robed women with long braids **(kore)** hold objects representing the gifts they bring to the gods. The naked men **(kouros)** may represent athletes, or gods, or a deceased ancestor. What they all have in common

Three-headed demon from the Hekatompedon   Archaic Gallery: gifts to the gods

is they're stiff and unrealistic, standing at attention with generic faces and mysterious smiles.

This was the style of the Archaic era (c. 700-480 BC) that preceded the Greek Golden Age: Men are generally naked (showing off buff and toned bodies); the bearded dudes are adults, and boys are beardless; and women are modestly clothed, with braided hair and pleated robes—essentially columns with breasts. Though these statues were once painted (some still show traces), they are a far cry from the lively Golden Age wonders we'll see from the Parthenon.

▶ *Of all the statues on the Acropolis, the most important were of the goddess most dear to Athenians—Athena. Halfway down the gallery, on the right, find a large statue of Athena, a robed woman carrying a snake. She's one statue of several in the triangular-shaped...*

❹ Pediment of the Archaios Naos

Athena, dressed in an ankle-length cloak, strides forward, brandishing a snake as she attacks a giant, who sprawls backward onto his bum. In this "Battle of the Gods and Giants," it was Athena, the goddess of wisdom, who wielded rational thought to overcome brute force.

And thanks to Athena, the city of Athens came to dominate its barbarian Greek neighbors. In gratitude, the Athenians began building a grand new temple to Athena to replace the Hekatompedon. These statues decorated the entrance.

But then came the event that changed Greece's history forever. When the Persians invaded Greece for the second time (in 480 BC), they looted Athens and burned the Acropolis' temples to the ground. It was a horrible tragedy, but it left the hilltop a blank canvas. And when Athens rebounded, they were determined to rebuild the Acropolis

Female kore statue with Archaic smile

Pensive Athena, dressed for battle

Nike lifts her leg to adjust her sandal.

better than ever as a symbol of rebirth. The centerpiece would be a brand-new temple to Athena—the Parthenon.

▶ *Continue another 20 steps to the middle of the room, where the* ❺ ***Kritios Boy*** *(c. 480 BC) seems to be stepping gracefully from Archaic stiffness into Greece's Golden Age. From this point on, we'll be viewing artifacts from those Golden Age buildings you can actually see today atop the Acropolis—the Propylaea, Erechtheion, and Parthenon.*

Continue to the end of the hall, and circle clockwise around the escalators. Find displays on the Propylaea, the grand entrance to the newly rebuilt Acropolis.

❻ Propylaea and Temple of Athena Nike

The **model of the Propylaea** (also spelled Propylaia) shows how this entrance gate once looked—a grand, steep staircase that led the visitor up, up, up, and then through majestic columns, to emerge atop the Acropolis.

As you climbed, you'd pass by the **Temple of Athena Nike** (the empty platform standing just in front, on the right side), built to honor the fierce goddess who brought Athens Nike (Victory). Ruins from that temple are displayed a few steps to the left of the model.

This U-shaped set of reliefs (c. 410 BC) formed the balustrade ringing the temple. See how naturally the winged goddess Nike goes about her business: adjusting her sandal, leading a bull to sacrifice, ascending a staircase, and so on.

Displayed nearby are more chunks of the Temple of Athena Nike. You'll see toes gripping rocks, windblown robes, and realistically twisted bodies—exuberant, life-filled carvings signaling Athens' emergence from the Persian War.

▶ *Near the Propylaea model—tucked behind the escalators—is something you won't want to miss. Standing all on their own, as if starring in their own revue on a beautifully lit stage, are the...*

❼ Caryatids from the Erechtheion

Here stand five of the original six lady-columns that once supported the roof of the prestigious Erechtheion temple. (The six on the Acropolis today are copies; the other original is in London's British Museum.) While the Parthenon was the Acropolis' showstopper, the cute little Erechtheion (see the **model** back near the escalators) was actually Athens' holiest temple, as it marked the exact spot where legend says Athens was born.

The six statues form a harmonious ensemble, yet each is unique. They were the finishing touch on the architect Mnesicles' final temple, and they sum up the balance and serenity of the Golden Age.

Despite their elegant appearance, these sculptures were structurally functional. Each has a column for legs, a capital-like hat, and buttressing locks of hair. The Caryatids were modeled on the famously upright women of Karyai, near Sparta, and now any female statue used as a column is called a "caryatid."

The original Erechtheion Caryatids—ravaged by time and pollution—retain their elegant dignity.

Time and the elements have ravaged these maidens. As recently as the 17th century (see the engravings), they had fragile arms holding ritual bowls for libations. Until the 1950s (before modern smog), their worn-down faces had crisp noses and mouths. In a half-century of Industrial Age pollution, they experienced more destruction than in the previous 2,000 years. But their future looks brighter now that they've been brought indoors out of the acidic air, cleaned up with a laser, and safely preserved for future generations. (For more on the Caryatids in their original location, see page 83.)

▸ *Now that we've seen some of the Acropolis' "lesser" treasures, let's head upstairs for the grand finale. Ride the escalators to the top floor.*

Level 3: The Parthenon

This floor features the collection of Parthenon structures, laid out the way they were on the original Parthenon. In fact, this floor has roughly the same dimensions as the Parthenon—228 feet long and 101 feet wide. The escalators deposit you "inside" this virtual Parthenon, in the temple's *cella*—the inner sanctum.

▸ *Start by getting acquainted with the Parthenon through the exhibits here in the cella.*

❽ Parthenon Exhibits

The **video** reconstructs the Parthenon before your eyes and also covers the Parthenon's 2,500-year history—including a not-so-subtle jab at how Lord Elgin got the marbles and made off with them to England.

The **model of the Parthenon** in its prime also shows the sculptures in their original locations. Learn the terminology: The triangular-shaped ensemble over the two ends are the pediment sculptures. Beneath that is a row of relief panels running around the building, called the metopes. There was another similar row of relief panels, called the frieze, located under the eaves (but unfortunately this model lacks the detail to show it).

The **model of the east pediment** (the one to the left as you face the escalator) shows the statues you'd see above the Parthenon's main entrance. In the center, at the very peak of the triangle, a tiny winged angel (Nike) is about to place the olive wreath of victory on Athena (carrying a shield). This was the crowning moment of the legendary event that put Athens on the map—the birth of Athena. Zeus (seated

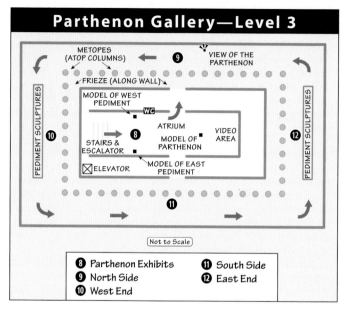

Parthenon Gallery—Level 3

METOPES
(ATOP COLUMNS)

9 VIEW OF THE
PARTHENON

FRIEZE (ALONG WALL)

MODEL OF WEST
PEDIMENT

WC

ATRIUM

MODEL OF
PARTHENON

VIDEO
AREA

PEDIMENT SCULPTURES

10

8

STAIRS &
ESCALATOR

ELEVATOR

MODEL OF EAST
PEDIMENT

PEDIMENT SCULPTURES

12

11

Not to Scale

8 Parthenon Exhibits	**11** South Side
9 North Side	**12** East End
10 West End	

on his throne) allowed Athena, the goddess of wisdom, to rise from his brain fully grown and fully armed, to inaugurate the Golden Age of Athens.

The drama and realism of these statues was incredible. Find powerful Poseidon (seated to the right with his trident), Apollo (with his lyre), and Aphrodite (reclining farther right). At the far left, Helios' four horses bring the sunrise, while four more (far right) bring sunset. Next to the sunrise horses (on the left), find Dionysus, just kicking back and chilling with another cup of wine. Try to remember how impressive these sculptures were in their prime, because—as you'll soon see—what remains today is mostly just fragments.

The **model of the west pediment** (on the opposite wall) shows Athena (with spear, shield, and spiky crown) competing with Poseidon for Athens' favor by giving gifts to the city. Athena won by presenting an olive tree (behind the two of them), which sprouted next to the

Parthenon. A big, heavenly audience looks on. Had Poseidon bested Athena, you'd be in Poseidonia today instead of Athens.

▶ *Now let's go see the sculptures—the pediments, metopes, and frieze—that once decorated the exterior of the Parthenon. We'll tour the floor counterclockwise. Facing the video screen, turn left and enter the huge outer gallery that rings the cella. (You'll be in the north gallery.) Step up to the window for a stunning* **view of the Parthenon**—*the temple that these sculptures once adorned. Now turn around and take in what remains.*

Parthenon Sculptures

This floor re-creates the dimensions (approximately) of the Parthenon. The stainless-steel columns mark the location of each marble column. The relief panels you see once ringed the Parthenon. The metopes (displayed higher up) formed a continuous band around the Parthenon's exterior. The frieze (mounted lower) also ran around the Parthenon's exterior, but inside the columned arcade. In their heyday, all these panels were originally painted in realistic colors.

The darker-brown panels are originals. The white plaster ones are copies of the originals in other museums. Even with copies, you'll notice there are a few gaps here and there, because some pieces have been lost forever and scholars don't know what was there.

We're lucky the Parthenon sculptures have survived as well as they did. It first had to suffer through 2,000 years exposed to the elements. Then, in 1687, the Parthenon was accidentally blasted to smithereens during a battle with the Ottomans. In 1801, Lord Elgin took the best of the shattered pieces back to London. Today, of the original marble frieze, the museum owns only 32 feet. These panels were already so acid-worn that Lord Elgin didn't bother taking them.

▶ *Start here on the...*

❾ North Side

Start with the museum's highlight—a life-size replica of the 525-foot **frieze** that once wrapped all the way around the outside of the Parthenon. It depicts the big parade of the Great Panathenaic Festival held every four years, when citizens climbed up the Acropolis to the Parthenon to celebrate the birth of their city.

The parade is in full swing. Chariots lumber in. Men lead animals

The third floor is laid out like the original Parthenon, with similar dimensions.

such as lambs and oxen to be sacrificed to the gods. At the heart of the procession are elegant maidens dressed in pleated robes. They shuffle along, carrying gifts for the gods on their shoulders, such as incense burners and jars of wine to pour out an offering. (There was one more gift for the gods that was the whole purpose of the parade—we'll come to that at the end.)

All the participants are heading in the same direction—uphill. Notice how, even though the horses gallop and rear back spiritedly, the men's gazes remain steady and form a harmonious line around the Parthenon.

Now turn to the **metopes.** Though pretty worn, these depict scenes of epic Greek contests—men battling monsters, gods battling giants, and superheroes of legend. The Greeks loved competition of all sorts, as it reflected the dynamic built into the cosmos. The panels on this side of the Parthenon depicted the epic struggles of the Trojan War. Find the lovely Helen who started it all, the brave Greek warrior Odysseus who wandered at war's end, and the hero on the losing team, Aeneas (five panels).

▶ *Head counterclockwise around the floor, turning the corner to the Parthenon's...*

⑩ West End

The sculptures here once decorated one of the Parthenon's two entrances. This was the temple's back door (though it's the iconic view that greets today's visitors).

The triangular-shaped **pediment** that once sat over the entrance (but which is now displayed on the ground) is pretty fragmentary and hard to make out. It once showed Athena in the center competing with Poseidon for Athens' affection (described earlier, under "Parthenon Exhibits").

The **metopes** are also pretty weathered (but at least they're originals). They depict another evenly matched contest—this time between Greek men and the legendary Amazons (on horseback).

The **frieze** picks up where we left off—the Panathenaic parade. Here, we have some of the museum's best scenes: Muscular horses with bulging veins are posed in every which way. Their riders' cloaks billow in the breeze as they gallop up the Acropolis. Some panels have holes drilled in them, where gleaming bronze reins were fitted to heighten the festive look.

▶ *Turn the corner to the other long side.*

⑪ South Side

The **metopes** here are some of the museum's finest. This is the legendary battle between men (the Lapiths) and half-horse centaurs. Follow the story, working right-to-left (starting at the far end of the hall): The centaurs have crashed a party (first three panels) to carry off the pleated-robed Lapith women. The Lapith men fight back (next six panels), but it's clear the centaurs are winning. Note the high-quality original metope (displayed on the ground for closer inspection) where a centaur has a man in a headlock and reaches back hoping to deliver the final blow. But the Lapiths rally (final two panels) and start to get the upper hand. For the Greeks, this contest symbolized how rational men had to constantly do battle to control his animalistic urges.

Now turn to the **frieze,** which seems to be picking up steam as we build to the parade's climax. It's a true celebration involving all of Athens: men on horseback, musicians, animals, priests, and dignitaries—all joining together on this festive anniversary of the birth of their great city. They're all headed to the Parthenon to present gifts to Athena.

▶ *The parade congregated around the Parthenon's entrance. Let's join them there. Continue around the bend to the east end, with some of the Parthenon's most famous statues.*

⑫ East End

These sculptures adorned the Parthenon's main entrance. Take a seat and see how the sculptures—pediment, frieze, and metopes—all culminate thematically here.

The **metopes** (though heavily damaged) illustrated the most primary myth in the Greek world: when the Olympian gods defeated the brutish Giants, thus creating the world of mortal men.

The **pediment** depicted the most important myth for the Athenians: the birth of Athena. (It's heavily damaged, with many gaps. Mentally fill them in with the model we saw in the entrance hallway on this floor, earlier.) The peak of the triangle (now missing) once

Scene from the 525-foot Parthenon frieze, depicting the Panathenaic parade up the Acropolis

showed Athena springing from Zeus' head, while the other gods reacted in astonishment. Of the pieces and copies here, you can make out Dionysus (reclining on the left), Aphrodite (lounging on the right), and the chess-set horse heads. The other figure is Hebe, the cupbearer of the gods, who seems to be hurrying to give Dionysus a refill.

The **frieze** depicts the culmination of the Panathenaic parade: when they arrive at the Parthenon and present their gifts. The most precious gift was a new robe (the *peplos*), woven by Athens' young girls. Find the robe in the central panel, where a man and a girl neatly fold the robe for presentation. Nearby, the gods look on approvingly, seated on their thrones. Athena, to the right, turns her back, apparently bored with the tiresome annual ritual.

In real life, the parade would congregate at the Parthenon entrance. Then a few chosen citizens would enter the temple and head to the inner sanctum (*cella*), where there was a 40-foot-tall wooden statue of Athena. They'd present the new robe to her, giving her thanks. Athena must have been pleased, as she made Athens the greatest city the Western world has known.

▶ *Finish your tour by strolling around the gallery again, reviewing the art, gazing out the windows, and taking a moment to...*

Ponder the Parthenon

There's the Parthenon itself, perched on the adjacent hilltop. Let the museum disappear around you, leaving you to enjoy the art and the temple it once decorated. The Parthenon is one of the most influential works humankind has ever created. For 2,500 years it's inspired generations of architects, sculptors, painters, engineers, and visitors from around the globe. Here in the Acropolis Museum, you can experience the power of this cultural landmark. The people of Athens relish the Acropolis Museum. They grow taller with every visit, knowing that Greece finally has a suitable place to preserve and share the best of its artistic heritage.

▶ *On your way down, stop by the restaurant on level 2 for its exterior terrace and the awesome view of the Acropolis, and consider touring the ancient excavations beneath the museum—accessed via a ramp back at the museum entrance (scan your ticket for entry).*

National Archaeological Museum Tour

Εθνικό Αρχαιο Λογικό Μουσείο

The National Archaeological Museum is the top ancient Greek art collection anywhere. Ancient Greece set the tone for all Western art that followed, and this museum lets you trace its evolution from 7000 BC to AD 500 through beautifully displayed and described exhibits on one floor. You'll see the rise and fall of Greece's various civilizations: the Minoans, the Mycenaeans, those of Archaic Greece, the Classical Age and Alexander the Great, and the Romans. Watch Greek sculpture evolve, from prehistoric Barbie dolls, to stiff Egyptian style, to the *David*-like balance of the Golden Age, to wet T-shirt, buckin'-bronco Hellenistic, and finally, to the influence of the Romans.

ORIENTATION

Cost: €10, €5 off-season.

Hours: Daily 8:00-20:00 except Tue from 12:30, Nov-March 9:00-16:00 (Tue from 12:30).

Information: Tel. 213-214-4800, www.namuseum.gr.

Getting There: The museum is a mile north of the Plaka at 28 Oktovriou (a.k.a. Patission) #44. Your best bet is to take a **taxi,** which costs about €6 from the Plaka. By **Metro,** use the Omonia stop (as you exit, follow signs to *28 Oktovriou/28 October street,* and walk seven blocks to the museum—about 15 minutes) or the Victoria stop (about a 10-minute walk). You can also hop a **bus:** A short walk north of Monastiraki is the Voreu (Βορεου, "North") stop, where you can catch bus #035; ride it to the Patission (Πατησιων) stop, a block in front of the museum. Or, from Syntagma Square (near the corner of the National Garden), catch bus #2, #4, #5, or #11 to Polytechneio (Πολυτεχνειο).

Tours: There are no audioguides, but live **guides** sometimes hang out in the lobby waiting to give you a €50, hour-long tour of hit-or-miss quality.

♫ Download my free National Archaeological Museum **audio tour.**

Length of This Tour: Allow at least two hours, more if you want to dig deeper into this world-class museum.

Baggage Check: Free and required, except for small purses.

Services: A museum shop, WCs, and an inviting café surround a shady and restful courtyard in the lower level (to access from the main entrance lobby, take the stairs down behind ticket desk); these are easiest to access at the beginning or end of your museum tour.

No-no's: Although photography is allowed, goofy poses in front of statues are not. The Greek museum board considers this disrespectful of the ancient culture and is very serious about it.

Starring: The gold Mask of Agamemnon, stately kouros and kore statues, the perfectly posed *Artemision Bronze,* the horse and jockey of Artemision, and the whole range of Greek art.

THE TOUR BEGINS

The collection is delightfully chronological. To sweep through Greek history, simply visit the numbered rooms in order. From the entrance lobby (Rooms 1-2), start with the rooms directly in front of you (Rooms 3-6), containing prehistoric and Mycenaean artifacts. Then circle clockwise around the building's perimeter (Rooms 7-33) to see the evolution of classical Greek statuary. Keep track of your ticket—you'll need it to enter or reenter some rooms.

Use the following self-guided tour for an overview, then browse to your heart's content, using the excellent information posted in each room.

▶ *From the entrance lobby, go straight ahead into the large central hall (Room 4). This first area—Rooms 3-6—is dedicated to prehistory (7000-1050 BC). Start in the small side room to the right, Room 6. In the display case directly to the right as you enter, you'll find stiff marble figures with large heads, known as...*

❶ Cycladic Figurines

Goddess, corpse, fertility figure, good-luck amulet, spirit guide, beloved ancestor, or Neolithic porn? No one knows for sure the purpose of these female figurines, which are older than the Egyptian pyramids. Although these statuettes were made only in the Cycladic Islands, well-traveled ones have been found all over Greece. The earliest Greeks may have worshipped a Great Mother earth goddess long before Zeus and company (variously called Gaia, Ge, and other names), but it's not clear what connection she had, if any, with these statuettes. The ladies are always naked, usually with folded arms. The

Cycladic figures—prehistoric Barbies?

Mask of Agamemnon—a Mycenaean treasure

National Archaeological Museum

41　42　43　44　47

37　36　45　46

40　37A

38

35

To ↓

23

34

39

17　18

11

16　To Café　**14**　PEDIMENT RELIEFS

& WCs　**13**

19　21　22　23　24

3　**4**　25

10　20

CLAY TABLETS　28

15　**12**　FRESCOES　WARRIOR KRATER　**15**

14　10　**3**　**16**

5　6

BASES　4　26　29

13　10　**2**　**17**

9　9　**1**　27

CAFÉ & WCs

To Café ←

& WCs　30

KOUROI　5　**19**

11　8　7　2　33　32　31　**18**

8　**7**　**6**　ROOM 1　**22**　**21**　**20**

12　30A

↑ ENTRANCE

VASIL. IRAKLEIOU

CAFÉ

To Ⓜ Victoria ←　To 28 Oktovriou (Patission)　To Plaka & Acropolis

28 OKTOVRIOU (PATISSION)

figures evolved over the years from flat-chested, to violin-shaped, to skinny. There is evidence that the eyes, lips, and ears were originally painted on.

▶ *To see the golden treasures of Mycenae, return to the long central hall (Room 4), which is divided into four sections. Here you'll find the...*

❷ Mask of Agamemnon and Other Mycenaean Treasures

Room 4 displays artifacts found in the ruins of the ancient fortress-city of Mycenae, 80 miles west of Athens. You're surrounded by 30 pounds of gold pounded into decorative funerary objects—swords, daggers, armor, and jewelry—all found buried alongside 19 bodies in a circle of Mycenaean graves. The objects' intricately hammered detail and the elaborate funeral arrangements point to the sophistication of this early culture.

In the glass case facing the entry door is the so-called **Mask of Agamemnon** (c. 1550 BC). Made of beaten gold and showing a man's bearded face, this famous mask was tied over the face of a dead man—note the tiny ear-holes for the string.

The Mycenaeans dominated southern Greece a thousand years before the Golden Age (1600-1200 BC). Their (real) history dates from the misty era of Homer's (fanciful) legends of the Trojan War. But in the 19th century, the ruins of the real-life Troy (in western Turkey) were unearthed. The archaeologist Heinrich Schliemann (the Indiana Johann of his era) suggested that the Mycenaeans were the Greeks who'd conquered Troy (which may be true). So Schliemann next excavated Mycenae and found this remarkable trove. He went on to declare this funeral mask to be that of the legendary Greek King Agamemnon, who conquered the Trojans. (Unfortunately, that part can't be true, because the mask predates the fall of Troy around 1300 BC.)

▶ *In the next section of Room 4, you'll find...*

❸ More Mycenaean Artifacts

A model of the Acropolis of Mycenae (left side) shows the dramatic hilltop citadel where many of these objects were unearthed. Also near the entrance to Room 4 are brightly colored **frescoes,** done in the style of the Mycenaeans' sophisticated neighbors, the Minoans (and featuring the Minoan sport of bull-jumping). At the end of this area, on the left, **clay tablets** show the Mycenaean written language known as Linear B, whose syllabic script (in which marks stand for syllables) was cracked only in the 1950s.

In the display case is Schliemann's favorite find—a painted, two-handled vase known as the **House of the Warrior Krater** (#1426). A woman (far left) waves goodbye to a line of warriors heading off to war, with their fancy armor and duffle bags hanging from their spears. This 3,000-year-old scene of Mycenaean soldiers is timeless, with countless echoes across the generations.

▶ *Continue to the last section of Room 4. In the center, a glass case displays the...*

❹ Vapheio Cups

These gold cups (c. 1600-1550 BC), found with other precious items in a Mycenaean tomb, are metalwork masterpieces. The intricate worked

Warrior Krater shows soldiers off to war.

Vapheio cup—beautiful bovine love

detail on #1 shows a charging bull sending a guy head over heels. On #2 you'll see a bull and a cow making eyes at each other, while the hind leg of another bull gets tied up by one good-looking cowboy. These realistic, joyous scenes are the product of the two civilizations that made 15th-century BC Greece the wonder of Europe—the Mycenaeans and the Minoan culture of Crete.

For four centuries (c. 1600-1200 BC), the warlike Mycenaeans dominated Greece. They were rich enough to hire accomplished Minoan artisans to paint their frescoes and decorate their cups. Then, suddenly—whether from invasion, famine, internal strife, or natural disaster—the Mycenaeans disappeared from history's radar screen. It plunged Greece into 500 years of Dark Ages (c. 1200-700 BC). Little survives from that chaotic time, so let's pick up the thread of history as Greece began to recover a few centuries later.

▶ *Backtrack to the entrance lobby, then turn right, and begin circling clockwise around the perimeter of the building, starting in Room 7. After scanning your ticket again to enter this room, look for the tall vase on your right.*

❺ Dipylon Vase

This monumental ocher-and-black vase (c. 750 BC) is painted with a funeral scene. In the center, the deceased lies on a funeral bier, flanked by a line of mourners who pull their hair in grief. It's far from realistic.

The Dipylon vase depicts stick-figure mourners tearing out their hair in grief.

The triangular torsos, square arms, circular heads, and bands of geometric patterns epitomize the style of what's known as the Geometric Period (9th-8th century BC). A few realistic notes pop through, such as the raw emotions of the mourners and some grazing antelope and ibex (on the neck of the vase).

This (relatively) sophisticated vase demonstrates that, after centuries of Dark Ages and war, the Greeks were beginning to settle down. They were establishing cities and expanding abroad (as seen on the map nearby). They were developing a written language and achieving the social stability that could afford to generate art. Next came large-scale statues in stone.

▶ *In Rooms 7-14 you'll get a look at some of these giant statues, including the early Greek statues called...*

Kore and Kouros

Some of the earliest surviving examples of post-Mycenaean Greek art (c. 700-480 BC) are these life-size and larger-than-life statues of clothed young women (kore/korai) and naked young men (kouros/kouroi). Influenced by ancient statues of Egyptian pharaohs, they're big and stiff, with triangular faces and arms at their sides. But as you walk through the next few rooms, you'll see the statues become increasingly more realistic and natural in their movements, with more personality.

▶ *Start with the statue facing the vase in the middle of Room 7, a...*

❻ **Kore** (c. 650 BC): With hands at her sides, a skinny figure, a rectangular shape, and dressed in a full-length robe (called a chiton), this kore looks as much like a plank of wood as a woman. Her triangular lion-mane hairstyle resembles an Egyptian headdress. The writing down her left leg says she's dedicated to Apollo.

▶ *In the next room (Room 8), your eyes go right to a very nice pair of knees that belong to a...*

❼ **Kouros from Sounion** (c. 600 BC): A typical kouros from the Archaic period, this young naked man has braided dreadlocks and a stable forward-facing pose, and is stepping forward slightly with his left leg. His fists are clenched at his sides, and his scarred face obscures an Archaic smile. His anatomy is strongly geometrical and stylized, with almond-shaped eyes, oval pecs, an arched rib cage,

Left to right: female statue #1, kouros from Sounion, kore with flower, kouros stepping out

cylindrical thighs, trapezoidal knees, and a too-perfect symmetry. While less plank-like than earlier statues, he's still much flatter than an actual person. The overdeveloped muscles (look at those quads!) and his narrow waist resemble those of an athletic teenager.

Rather than strict realism, kouros statues capture a geometric ideal. The proportions of the body parts follow strict rules—for example, most later kouros statues are precisely seven "heads" tall. Although this kouros steps forward slightly, his hips remain even (think about it—the hips of a real person would shift forward on one side). The Greeks were obsessed with the human body—remember, these statues were of (idealized) humans, not gods. Standing naked and alone, these statues represented a microcosm of the rational order of nature.

Statues were painted in vivid, lifelike colors. But the rough surface lacks the translucent sheen of Classical Age statues, because

Archaic chisels were not yet strong enough for the detail work without cracking the marble.

Kouros statues were everywhere, presented as gifts to a god at a sanctuary or to honor the dead in a cemetery. This one was dedicated to Poseidon at the entrance to the temple at Sounion. As a funeral figure, a kouros symbolized the deceased in his prime of youth and happiness, forever young.

▶ *Continue into the next room (Room 11). On the left, holding a flower, is a...*

❽ **Kore** (c. 550 BC): Where a male kouros was naked and either life-size or larger than life (emphasizing masculine power), a female kore was often slightly smaller than life and modestly clothed, capturing feminine grace (males were commonly naked in public, but women never were). This petite kore stands with feet together, wearing a pleated chiton belted at the waist. Her hair is braided and held in place with a diadem (a wreath-like headdress), and she wears a necklace. Her right hand tugs at her dress, indicating motion (a nice trick if the artist lacks the skill to actually show it), while her left hand holds a flower. Like most ancient statues, she was painted in lifelike colors, including her skin. Her dress was red—you can still see traces of the paint—adorned with flower designs and a band of swastikas down the front. (In ancient times the swastika was a harmless good-luck symbol representing the rays of the sun.) This kore, like all the statues in the room, has that distinct Archaic smile (or smirk, as the Greeks describe it). Browse around. Study the body types—the graceful, *Avatar*-like builds, those mysterious smirks, and the rigid hairdos.

▶ *The next room—a long hall labeled Room 13—has...*

❾ **More Kouroi:** These statues, from the late Archaic period (around 500 BC), once decorated the tombs of hero athletes—perhaps famous Olympians. Notice that these young men are slightly more relaxed and realistic, with better-formed thighs and bent elbows.

Farther down Room 13 (left side), find the two square marble **Bases for Funerary Kouroi.** These were pedestals for kouros statues of the deceased. The carved reliefs are yet another baby step in the artistic march toward realism. On the first base, the relief shows wrestlers and other athletes, with remarkably realistic twisting poses. Around the right side, notice the cute dog-and-cat fight. The second

The Four Stages of Greek Sculpture

Archaic (c. 700-480 BC): Rigid statues with stylized anatomy, facing forward, with braided hair and mysterious smiles.

Severe (c. 480-460 BC): More realistic and balanced statues (with no smiles), capturing a serious nobility. Works from this transitional period are sometimes described as Early Classical.

Classical (c. 460-323 BC): Realistic statues of idealized beauty with poses that strike a balance between movement and stillness, with understated emotion. (Within this period, the Golden Age was roughly 450-400 BC.)

Hellenistic (c. 323-30 BC): Photorealistic (even ugly) humans engaged in dramatic, emotional struggles, captured in snapshot poses that can be wildly unbalanced.

base features a field hockey-like game, each scene reflecting the vigor of the deceased man in his prime.

During the Archaic period, Greece was prospering, growing, expanding, trading, and colonizing the Mediterranean. The smiles on the statues capture the bliss of a people settling down and living at peace. But in 480 BC, Persia invaded, and those smiles soon vanished.

▶ *Pass through Room 14 and into Room 15, which is dominated by one of the jewels of the collection, the...*

⑩ *Artemision Bronze*

This statue was discovered amid a shipwreck off Cape Artemision (north of Athens) in 1928. The weapon was never found, so no one knows for sure if this is Zeus or Poseidon. The god steps forward, raises his arm, sights along his other arm at the distant target, and prepares to hurl his thunderbolt (if it's Zeus) or his trident (if it's Poseidon).

The god stands 6'10" and has a physique like mine. His hair is curly and tied at the back, and his now-hollow eyes once shone white with inset bone. He plants his left foot and pushes off with the right. Even though every limb moves in a different direction, the whole effect is one of balance. The statue's dimensions are a study in Greek geometry. His head is one Greek foot high, and he's six heads tall (or one

Greek fathom). The whole figure has an "X" shape that would fit into a perfect circle, with his navel at the center and his fingertips touching the rim. Although the bronze statue—cast with the "lost wax" technique (explained later, under *"Artemision Jockey"*)—is fully three-dimensional, it's most impressive from the front. (Later Greek statues, from the Hellenistic era, seem fully alive from every angle, including the three-quarter view.)

This Zeus/Poseidon, from c. 460 BC, is an example of the transition into the Classical style, as sculpture evolved beyond the so-called Severe style (480-460 BC). Historically, the Severe/Early Classical Period covers the time when Greece battled the Persians and emerged victorious—the era when ordinary men had also just shaken off tyrants and taken control of their own destiny through democracy. The Greeks were entering the dawn of the Golden Age. During this time of horrific war, the Greeks made art that was serious (no more Archaic smiles), unadorned, and expressed the noble strength and heroism of the individuals who had carried them through tough times. The statues are anatomically realistic, celebrating the human form.

With his movements frozen, as if Zeus/Poseidon were posing for a painting, we can examine the wonder of the physical body. He's natural yet ideal, twisting yet balanced, moving while at rest. (Later Greek sculptures would improve upon this, with figures that look almost as if they've been caught mid-motion with the click of a camera.) With his geometrical perfection and godlike air, the figure sums up all that is best about the art of the ancient world.

▶ *Continue into Room 16, filled with big marble vases labeled* ⓫ **Attic Funerary Monuments.** *These grave markers take the shape of the ceramic urns used for the ashes of cremated bodies. Vase #4485 is particularly touching: A grieving family looks on as Hermes (with his winged sandals) leads a young woman to the underworld.*

Continue into Room 17, then turn right into Room 19. (Note that the WCs and café are out the door ahead of you.) But for now, turn right in Room 19, then hook left into Room 20. At the far end of this room is item #129, the...

⓬ *Athena Varvakeion*

This marble statue (c. AD 250) is considered the most faithful copy of the great *Athena Parthenos* (438 BC) by Pheidias. It's essentially a

The 6'10" bronze god is frozen at the exact moment he's set to hurl his weapon.

one-twelfth-size replica of the 40-foot statue that once stood in the Parthenon. Although a miniature copy of the glorious original, it provides a good introduction to Greek art at its Golden Age pinnacle. Athena stands dressed in flowing robes, holding a small figure of Nike (goddess of victory) in her right hand and a shield in her left. Athena's helmet sprouts plumes with winged horses and a sphinx. To give a sense of scale of the original, the tiny Nike in Athena's hand was six feet tall in the Parthenon statue. Athena is covered in snakes. She wears a snake belt and bracelet; coiled snakes decorate her breastplate and one is curled up inside her shield, representing the goddess' connection to her half-snake son, who was born out of the earth and considered to be one of the ancestors of the Athenians. The snake-headed Medusa (whom Athena helped Perseus slay) adorns the center of her chest.

▶ *Backtrack to Room 17, turn right, and continue circling the museum clockwise into Room 18, which has…*

⑬ Funeral *Steles*

The tombstones that fill this room, all from the fifth century BC, are more good examples of Golden Age Greek art. With a mastery of the body, artists show poignant scenes of farewell, as loved ones bid a sad goodbye to the dead, who are seated. The tombstone in the center of the room depicts a rich woman pondering which treasure from her jewel box to take with her into eternity. On the left wall, a woman who died in childbirth looks at her baby, held by a servant as it reaches for its dead mother. Other scenes include a beautiful young woman, who died in her prime, narcissistically gazing into a mirror. Servants are shown taking part in the sad event, as if part of the family.

Small-scale version of 40-foot Athena

Funeral *stele*—a mother mourns her baby.

Though shallow reliefs, these works are effectively three-dimensional. There's a timeless melancholy in the room, a sense that no matter who you are—or how rich—when you go, you go alone...and shrouds have no pockets.

▶ *Pass into Room 21, a large central hall. We'll take a temporary break from the chronological sequence to see statues dating from the second century BC, when Greece was ruled by Rome. The hall is dominated by the...*

⑭ *Artemision Jockey*

In this bronze statue (c. 140 BC), the horse is racing in full stride, as a young jockey hangs on for dear life. The statue was recovered in pieces from the seafloor off Cape Artemision. Missing were the reins the jockey once held in his left hand and the whip he used with his right to spur the horse to go even faster—maybe too fast, judging by the look on his face.

Greeks loved their horse races, and this statue may celebrate a victory at one of the Panhellenic Games. The jockey is dressed in a traditional short tunic, has inlaid eyes, and his features indicate that he was probably ethnically part Ethiopian.

The statue, like other ancient bronzes, was made not by hammering sheets of metal, but with the classic "lost wax" technique. The artist would first make a rough version of the statue from clay, cover it with a layer of wax, and then cover that with another layer of clay to make a form-fitting mold. When heated in a furnace to harden the mold, the wax would melt—or be "lost"—leaving a narrow space between the clay model and the mold. The artist would then pour molten bronze into the space, let it cool, break the mold, and—*voilà!*—end up with a hollow bronze statue. This particular statue was cast in pieces, which were then welded together. After the cast was removed, the artist added a few surface details and polished it smooth. Notice the delightful detail on the rider's spurs, which were lashed to his bare feet.

The other statues in the room are second-century BC Roman copies of fifth-century BC Greek originals. Thanks to excellent copies like the ones in this room, we know what many (otherwise lost) Golden Age Greek masterpieces looked like. (By the way, when the Romans tried to re-create a bronze statue in marble, they often added

Horse and jockey—unbridled emotion

Realistic grave relief

extra support. So if you see a tree trunk buttressing some statue, it's likely a Roman copy.)

▶ *But, with the Romans, we're getting ahead of ourselves. To pick up where we left off (in the Golden Age), head straight past the jockey into Room 22 (with pediment reliefs). Then pass through a couple of rooms displaying funeral monuments until you reach the long Room 28, where you'll come face-to-face with a large...*

⑮ Grave Relief of a Horse

The spirited horse steps lively and whinnies while an Ethiopian boy struggles with the bridle and tries to calm him with food. The realistic detail of the horse's muscles and veins is astonishing, offset by the panther-skin blanket. The horse's head pops out of the relief, becoming fully three-dimensional. The boy's pose is slightly off-balance, anticipating the "unposed poses" of later Hellenism (this relief is from the late fourth century BC). We sense the emotions of both the overmatched boy and the nervous horse. We also see a balance between the horse and boy, with the two figures creating a natural scene together rather than standing alone.

▶ *Farther down Room 28 stands the impressive, slightly-larger-than-life-size...*

⑯ Bronze Statue of a Youth

Scholars can't decide whether this statue (c. 340-330 BC) is reaching out to give someone an apple or demonstrating a split-finger fastball. He may be Perseus, holding up the head of Medusa, but he's most likely the mythical Paris, awarding a golden apple to the winner of a beauty contest between goddesses (sparking jealousies that started the Trojan War).

The figure is caught in mid-step as he reaches out, gazing intently at the person he's giving the object to. Split this youth vertically down the middle to see the *contrapposto* (or "counter-poise") stance of so many Classical statues. His left foot is stable, while the right moves slightly, causing his hips to shift. Meanwhile, his right arm is tense while the left hangs loose. These subtle, contrary motions are in perfect balance around the statue's vertical axis.

In the Classical Age, statues reached their peak of natural realism and balanced grace. During the following Hellenistic Period, sculptors added to that realism, injecting motion and drama. Statues are fully three-dimensional (and Hellenistic statues even more so, as they have no "front": You have to walk around them to see the whole picture). Their poses are less rigid than those in the Archaic period and less overtly heroic than those of the Severe. The beauty of the face, the perfection of the muscles, the balance of elegant grace and brute power—these represent the full ripeness of the art of this age.

▶ *Continue into the small Room 29. To the left of the next doorway, find a black bronze head in a glass case. Look into the wild and cynical inlaid eyes of this...*

⑰ Head from a Statue of a Philosopher

This philosopher was a Cynic, part of a movement of nonmaterialist nonconformists founded in the fourth century BC by Diogenes. The term "cynic" aptly describes these guys with unkempt hair who questioned their society's obsessions with wealth and status. The statue's

Bronze youth—perfectly balanced grace

Philosopher, a Hellenist individual

aged, bearded face captures the personality of a distinct individual and is considered a portrait of a real-life person.

From c. 240 BC, it's typical of the Hellenistic Period, the time after the Macedonian Alexander the Great conquered Greece and spread Greek culture across the Mediterranean world. Hellenistic Greek society celebrated individualism and everyday people like this. Rather than Photoshop out their eccentricities, they presented their subjects warts and all. For the first time in history, we see human beings in all their gritty human glory: with wrinkles, male-pattern baldness, saggy boobs, and middle-age spread, all captured in less-than-noble poses.

The glass case to the left shows other parts of his body. The statue was likely shipped in pieces (like an Ikea self-assembly kit) for practical purposes.

This statue, like a number of the museum's statues, was found by archaeologists on the seabed off the coast of Greece. Where the wreck off Cape Artemision gave us Zeus/Poseidon and the bronze horse, another wreck (off the Greek mainland's southern tip) yielded this statue and the bronze youth (depicting Paris/Perseus).

▶ *Continue into the long Room 30 and head to the far end to find the…*

⓲ Statue of a Fighting Gaul

Having been wounded in the thigh (note the hole), this soldier has fallen to one knee and reaches up to fend off the next blow. The style of his helmet indicates that he's not a Greek, but a Gaul (from ancient France). The artist catches the exact moment when the tide of battle is about to turn. The face of this Fighting Gaul says he's afraid he may become the Dying Gaul.

The statue (c. 100 BC) sums up many of the features of Hellenistic art: He's frozen in motion in a wild, unbalanced pose that dramatizes his inner thoughts. The diagonal pose runs up his left leg and out his head and outstretched arm. Rather than a noble, idealized god, this is an ordinary soldier caught in an extreme moment. His arms flail, his muscles strain, his eyes bulge, and he cries out in pain. This statue may have been paired with others in a theatrical mini-drama that heightened emotion. Hellenism shows us the thrill of victory, and—in this case—the agony of defeat.

▶ *To the right, on the other side of a doorway, is a…*

Fighting Gaul with unbalanced pose

Aphrodite, Pan, and Eros flirting

⑲ Statue of Aphrodite, Pan, and Eros

In this playful marble ensemble (c. 100 BC) from the sacred island of Delos, Aphrodite is about to whack Pan with her sandal. Striking a classic *contrapposto* pose (with most of her weight on one foot), Aphrodite is more revealing than modest, her voluptuous body polished smooth. There's a bit of whimsy here, as Aphrodite seems to be saying, "Don't! Stop!"...but may instead be saying, "Don't stop." The actions of the (literally) horny Pan can also be interpreted in two ways: His left arm is forceful, but his right is gentle—holding her more like a dance partner. Eros, like an omnipresent Tinkerbell, comes to Aphrodite's aid—or does he? He has the power to save her if she wants help, but with a hand on Pan's horn and a wink, Eros seems to say, "OK, Pan, this is your chance. Come on, man, go for it." Pan can't believe his luck. This marble is finer than those used in earlier statues, and it has been polished to a sheen with an emery stone. As you walk around this delightful statue, enjoy the detail, from the pudgy baby feet and the remnants of red paint on the sandal to the way the figures all work together in a cohesive vignette.

▶ *Now, enter Room 31 to see a...*

⑳ Statue of the Emperor Augustus

This statue of Augustus introduces us to the next great era of ancient Greece—as a part of the vast Roman Empire. Augustus, the adopted son of Julius Caesar, was the founder of the Roman Empire and its first emperor (c. 12-10 BC). This is the only known statue of him on horseback, although it is missing its lower half. He holds the (missing) reins in his left hand and raises his right hand in a gesture of blessing or of oration—an expression of the emperor's power.

Emperor Augustus and the Romans conquered Greece, but they succumbed to Greek culture.

Although Greece was conquered by Rome, Greek culture ultimately "conquered" the Romans. The Romans were great warriors, engineers, and administrators, but they had an inferiority complex when it came to art. Grecophile Romans imported Greek statues and cranked out high-quality copies to beautify their villas. As Augustus remade the city of Rome, he used Greek-style columns and crossbeams—a veneer of sophistication on buildings erected with no-nonsense, brick-and-concrete Roman-arch engineering. It's largely thanks to the Romans and their respect for Greek culture that so much of this ancient art survives today.

▶ *For more Roman-era art, step into Room 32 and find a portrait of a beautiful woman asleep on a rock.*

㉑ Sleeping Maenad (and Friends)

In the center of the room is a marble statue (c. AD 120) featuring a sleeping Maenad, a female follower of the god Dionysus. Like a sleeping beauty, this slumbering Maenad lies exposed atop a rock on a soft skin of a panther.

Nearby, find a bust of **Hadrian.** This Roman emperor not only loved Greek culture, but he also had a hunky young Greek boyfriend named Antinous. To Hadrian's left is a fine portrait bust that may depict **Antinous** (or is it Channing Tatum?). After the young man drowned in the Nile in AD 130, the depressed Hadrian had him deified and commissioned statues of him throughout the empire.

▶ *Although Greece flourished under the Romans, their time was coming to an end. Continue into Room 33 to see...*

㉒ **Busts from the Late Roman Empire**

These busts (AD 300-500) capture the generic features and somber expressions of the late Roman Empire. As Rome decayed and fell to barbarians, ancient culture and artwork went into steep decline. The empire shifted its capital eastward to Constantinople (modern Istanbul). For the next thousand years, the Byzantine Empire, which included Greece, lived on as an enlightened, Christian, Greek-speaking enclave, while Western Europe fell into poverty and ignorance. During that time, ancient Greek culture was buried under centuries of rubble. Then, during the Renaissance (c. 1500), there was a renewed interest in the glory of ancient Greece. Gradually, Greek sites were unearthed, its statues cleaned up and repaired, and Greek culture once again was revived in all its inspirational glory.

▶ *Exit into the entrance lobby and take a breath. If you have an appetite for more, consider one more stop: some colorful frescoes as old as Stonehenge but as fresh as today. To get there, return to the boy on the horse. Behind the horse (in Rooms 34-35), find the grand ㉓* **staircase.** *Climb to the top of the stairs, continue straight into Room 48, and go to the far end of the room to find...*

Cycladic Wall Paintings: These are a product of the first great Greek civilization—the Minoans. These murals once decorated the walls of homes at Akrotiri on the island of Santorini (Thira). Akrotiri's people shared an artistic tradition with the Minoans, and they were among the first to love beauty for its own sake. That love of beauty became part of the legacy of ancient Greece.

▶ *Our tour is over. It's time to leave the ancients and make your way back to central Athens and the modern world.*

Sights

Compared to Europe's other big cities, Athens is relatively light on things to do and see. But the few major sights it does have are big-time. The main ones—the Acropolis, Ancient Agora, Acropolis Museum, and National Archaeological Museum—are described in detail in their individual chapters. There you'll find self-guided tours, plus tips on how to avoid lines and save money. Other attractions, including churches and less-prominent ancient sites, are also covered in greater depth in my Athens City Walk. If there's more information on a sight elsewhere, it's marked with a 📖. A 🎧 means the walk or tour is available as a free audio tour (via my Rick Steves Audio Europe app—see sidebar on page 11).

Be aware that open hours at some sights may vary from those printed in this book. Check locally before planning your day.

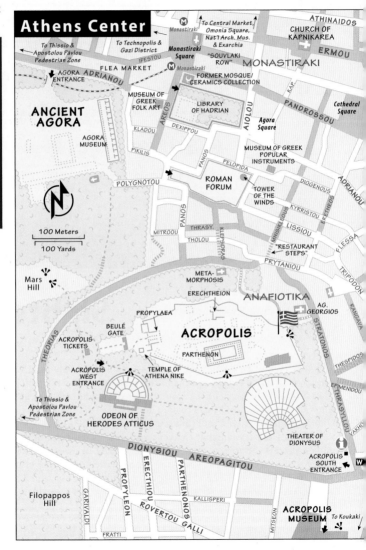

Athens Center

To Thissio &
Apostolou Pavlou
Pedestrian Zone

To Technopolis &
Gazi District

Monastiraki

To Central Market,
Omonia Square,
Nat'l Arch. Mus.
& Exarchia

ATHINAIDOS

CHURCH OF
KAPNIKAREA

ERMOU

IFESTOU

Monastiraki
Square

"SOUVLAKI
ROW"

MONASTIRAKI

FLEA MARKET

Monastiraki

AGORA ADRIANOU

AGORA
ADRIANOU
ENTRANCE

FORMER MOSQUE/
CERAMICS COLLECTION

MUSEUM OF
GREEK FOLK
ART

LIBRARY
OF HADRIAN

AREOS

AIOLOU

KAP.

PANDROSSOU

Cathedral
Square

ANCIENT
AGORA

KLADOU

DEXIPPOU

Agora
Square

Cathedral
Square

AGORA
MUSEUM

PIKILIS

PANOS

PELOPIDA

MUSEUM OF GREEK
POPULAR
INSTRUMENTS

DIOGENOUS

ADRIANOU

POLYGNOTOU

ROMAN
FORUM

TOWER
OF THE
WINDS

KYRRISTOU

RETHEOS

LISSIOU

FLESSA

PANOS

MITROOU

THRASY.

THOLOU

KLEPSIDRAS

"RESTAURANT
STEPS"

PRYTANIOU

TRIPODON

100 Meters

100 Yards

Mars
Hill

META-
MORPHOSIS

ERECHTHEION

ANAFIOTIKA

AG.
GEORGIOS

KANGAVA

PROPYLAEA

ACROPOLIS

THEORIAS

BEULÉ
GATE

STRATONOS

ACROPOLIS
TICKETS

PARTHENON

THESPIDOS

ACROPOLIS
WEST
ENTRANCE

TEMPLE OF
ATHENA NIKE

EPIMENIDOU

To Thissio &
Apostolou Pavlou
Pedestrian Zone

ODEON OF
HERODES ATTICUS

THRASYLLOU

YAKHO

THEATER OF
DIONYSUS

ACROPOLIS
SOUTH
ENTRANCE

W

DIONYSIOU AREOPAGITOU

ERECTHIOU

PROPYLEON

PARTHENONOS

ROVERTOU
GALLI

KALLISPERI

MITSEON

ACROPOLIS
MUSEUM

To Koukaki

Filopappos
Hill

GARIVALDI

FRATTI

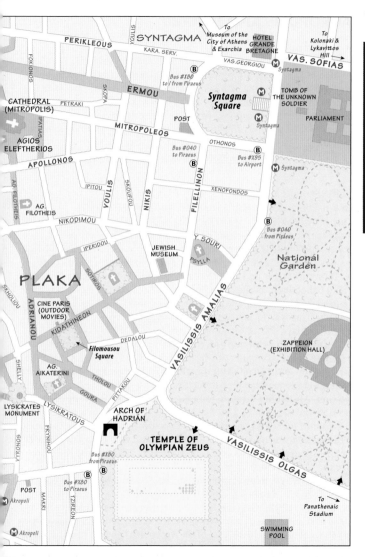

ACROPOLIS AND NEARBY

▲▲▲Acropolis

The most important ancient site in the Western world, the Acropolis (which means "high city" in Greek) rises gleaming like a beacon above the sprawl of modern Athens. Your Acropolis ticket also includes access to the scant remains of the **Theater of Dionysus,** scattered southeast of the Acropolis, just above the Dionysiou Areopagitou walkway (and only possible to visit in conjunction with your Acropolis entrance).

📖 See the Acropolis Tour chapter or 🎧 download my free audio tour.

▲▲"Acropolis Loop"
(a.k.a. Dionysiou Areopagitou and Apostolou Pavlou)

One of Athens' best attractions, this wide, well-manicured, delightfully traffic-free pedestrian boulevard borders the Acropolis to the south and west. It's composed of two streets with tongue-twisting names—Dionysiou Areopagitou and Apostolou Pavlou (think of them as Dionysus Street and Apostle Paul's Street); for simplicity, I refer to them collectively as the "Acropolis Loop." One of the city's many big upgrades from hosting the 2004 Olympics, this walkway immediately became a favorite local hangout, with vendors, al fresco cafés, and frequent special events enlivening its cobbles.

Dionysiou Areopagitou, wide and touristy, runs along the southern base of the Acropolis. It was named for Dionysus the Areopagite, first bishop and patron saint of Athens and a member of the ancient Roman-era senate that met atop Mars Hill (described next). The other section, **Apostolou Pavlou**—quieter, narrower, and tree-lined—curls around the western end of the Acropolis and the Ancient Agora. It feels more local and has the best concentration of outdoor eateries. This section was named for the Apostle Paul, who presented himself before Dionysus the Areopagite at Mars Hill. (To view the full "loop," see the "Athens" map on page 4.)

Where Apostolou Pavlou meets the Thissio Metro stop, you can head west on Ermou—a similarly enjoyable pedestrianized boulevard—to reach the Gazi district and the Keramikos Cemetery. If you head east on Ermou (with traffic), you'll come to Syntagma Square. Or, if you want to encircle the base of the Acropolis, head east on Adrianou,

Acropolis Tickets

A **basic Acropolis ticket** costs €20 (€10 Nov-March) and covers entry to the Acropolis, as well as access to sights on the north and south slopes, including the Theater of Dionysus. You can save time by purchasing your ticket at the south entrance ticket office rather than the often-crowded main (west entrance) Acropolis ticket office.

If you plan to visit Athens' other major ancient sites, the €30 **Acropolis combo-ticket** is the better deal, as it covers not only the Acropolis and Theater of Dionysus, but also the Ancient Agora (€8), Roman Forum (€6), Temple of Olympian Zeus (€6), Library of Hadrian (€4), and Keramikos Cemetery (€8; individual entry prices are cut in half for all of these sights in winter; no winter discount on combo-ticket). The combo-ticket is valid for five days, and since you can buy it at any participating sight, it allows you to skip the ticket-buying line at the Acropolis. Note that the Acropolis combo-ticket has one designated stub for the Acropolis, but all the others are interchangeable, so you can visit each covered sight once, or the same one several times.

These sights are always free for those 18 and under. They're also free on national holidays, and on the first Sunday of the month from November through March.

the pedestrian street you'll hit just before the Thissio Metro stop, and stroll through the Plaka on your way back to Dionysiou Areopagitou.

▲Mars Hill (Areopagus)

The knobby, windswept hill crawling with tourists in front of the Acropolis is Mars Hill, also known as Areopagus (from *Areios Pagos,* "Ares Hill," referring to the Greek version of Mars). While the views from the Acropolis are more striking, rugged Mars Hill (near the Acropolis' main entrance, at the western end) makes a pleasant perch. As you're climbing Mars Hill, be warned: The stone stairs (and the top of the rock) have been polished to a slippery shine by history and can be treacherous even when dry. Watch your step and use the metal staircase.

This hill has an interesting history. After Rome conquered Athens in 86 BC, the Roman overlords wisely decided to extend citizenship to any free man born here. (The feisty Greeks were less likely to rise up against a state that had made them citizens.) Whereas Rome called the shots on major issues, minor matters of local governance were determined on this hill by a gathering of leaders. During this time, the Apostle Paul—the first great Christian missionary and author of about half of the New Testament—preached to the Athenians here on Mars Hill. Paul looked out over the Agora and started talking about an altar he'd seen—presumably in the Agora (though archaeologists can't confirm)—to the "Unknown God." (A plaque embedded in the rock near the stairs contains the Greek text of Paul's speech.) Although the Athenians were famously open-minded, Paul encountered a skeptical audience and only netted a couple of converts (including Dionysus the Areopagite—the namesake of the pedestrian drag behind the Acropolis). Paul moved on to Corinth, where he enjoyed a better reception.

▲▲▲Acropolis Museum

Located at the foot of Athens' famous ancient hill, this modern-day temple to the Acropolis contains relics from Greece's most famous sight.

📖 See the Acropolis Museum Tour chapter.

▲Arch of Hadrian

This stoic triumphal arch stands at the edge of the new suburb of ancient Athens built by the Roman Emperor Hadrian in the second century AD.

📖 See the Athens City Walk chapter or 🎧 download my free audio tour.

▲▲Temple of Olympian Zeus

Started by an overambitious tyrant in the sixth century BC, this giant temple was not completed until Hadrian took over seven centuries later. Now 15 of the original 104 Corinthian columns stand evocatively over a ruined base in a field. You can get a good view of the temple ruins through the fence by the Arch of Hadrian, but if you have the Acropolis combo-ticket, consider dropping in for a closer look.

📖 See the Athens City Walk chapter or 🎧 download my free audio tour.

ANCIENT AGORA AND BEYOND

For locations of these sights, see the "Athens" map on page 4.

▲▲▲Ancient Agora: Athens' Market

Although literally and figuratively overshadowed by the impressive Acropolis, the Agora was for eight centuries the true meeting place of the city—a hive of commerce, politics, and everyday bustle.

📖 See the Ancient Agora Tour chapter or 🎧 download my free audio tour.

▲Thissio and Gazi

These trendy zones, each just a short walk west of the Agora down the main pedestrian drag, have a thriving passel of cafés and restaurants (some with Acropolis views). If you stroll around the "Acropolis Loop," you'll wander right past **Thissio;** consider stopping off for a meal, a drink, or just to poke around. Thissio also has an appealing open-air cinema (for details, see the Activities chapter).

Gazi, with hopping nightclubs and street festivals, huddles around the **Technopolis** events-center complex, built in the remains

Great nightlife and views in Thissio

of a 19th-century gas works. Technopolis hosts an eclectic assortment of cultural happenings, including art exhibits, rock concerts, and experimental theater (Pireos 100, Metro: Keramikos—as you exit, walk to the square brick smokestacks, https://athens-technopolis.gr).

Benaki Museum of Islamic Art

Sometimes it seems the Greeks would rather just forget the Ottoman chapter of their past...but when you're talking about nearly 400 years, that's difficult to do. If you're intrigued by what Greeks consider a low point in their history, pay a visit to this branch of the Benaki Museum. The 8,000-piece collection, displayed in two renovated Neoclassical buildings, includes beautifully painted ceramics, a rare 14th-century astrolabe, and an entire marble room from a 17th-century Cairo mansion.

▶ €9; Thu-Sun 10:00-18:00, closed Mon-Wed; northeast of Keramikos Cemetery at Agion Asomaton 22, at the corner with Dipilou, Metro: Thissio, tel. 210-325-1311, www.benaki.gr.

Keramikos Cemetery

Named for the ceramics workshops that used to surround it, this is a vast place to wander among marble tombstones from the seventh century BC onward. While the sprawling cemetery requires a good imagination to take on much meaning, the small, modern museum is a delight.

▶ €8, covered by Acropolis combo-ticket; daily 8:00-20:00, Oct until 18:00, Nov-March until 15:00 and closed Mon; Ermou 148, Metro stops: Thissio or Keramikos, tel. 210-346-3552.

THE PLAKA, MONASTIRAKI, AND SYNTAGMA

Between the Plaka and Monastiraki Square

These sights are covered in more detail in the 📖 Athens City Walk chapter and 🎧 my free audio tour.

▲Roman Forum (a.k.a. "Roman Agora") and Tower of the Winds

After the Romans conquered Athens in 86 BC, they quickly filled in the original Agora with monumental buildings. Then, they expanded

100 yards east to build their own version of an agora—an open space or forum—where people came to do business. Today it's a pile of ruins, watched over by the marvelously intact Tower of the Winds. Although you can see virtually the entire site for free from the hillside, going inside yields a closer look (the entry gate is at the west end near the tallest standing colonnade).

You'll enter through four colossal Doric columns, part of a **gateway** built by Emperor Augustus (c. 11 BC). The inscription in Greek says it was generously financed by his adoptive father, Julius Caesar, and dedicated to Athens' favorite goddess, Athena. You'll emerge into a vast open-air **courtyard** (100 x 120 yards) where Romans and Athenians gathered to shop and schmooze. The courtyard was surrounded by rows of columns, creating a shaded arcade housing businesses. On the right side was a bubbling fountain.

The 40-foot-tall, octagonal **Tower of the Winds** was an observatory, with a weathervane on top, sundials on its sides, and a clock powered by water within. Inside is a big round (and still-not-fully-understood) stone in the pavement with markings like a clock dial. The holes indicate that some device was mounted on top—perhaps a set of metal gears. As water flowed down from the Acropolis it was channeled into the narrow groove you see here. The water powered the gears, which turned the hands of the clock to show the time of day. Additional hands (turning at much slower speeds) could show the day of the year, the month of the zodiac, and so on.

To the right of the Tower of the Winds is a gray-stone-paved area with broken columns—all that remains of the Agora's **other monumental entrance.** The **two arches** nearby may have marked the offices of the market's quality-control inspectors. To the left of the Tower is a rectangular area surrounded by a ditch. It has a few remaining stone benches with toilet-seat holes in them, making it clear what this once was: the Agora's **public restroom.**

▸ *€6, covered by Acropolis combo-ticket; daily 8:00-20:00, shorter hours off-season; corner of Pelopida and Aiolou streets, Metro: Monastiraki, tel. 210-324-5220.*

Library of Hadrian

About a block from the Roman Forum, down Aiolou street, is an area of Roman ruins containing what's left of the Library of Hadrian (erected

AD 131-132), along with a few remains of various churches that were built in later periods.

Churches in the Center

These churches are covered in more detail in the 📖 Athens City Walk chapter and 🎧 my free audio tour.

▲Church of Kapnikarea

Sitting unassumingly in the middle of Ermou street, this small 11th-century Byzantine church offers a convenient look at the Greek Orthodox faith.

Cathedral (Mitropolis)

Dating from the mid-19th century, this is the big head church of Athens—and therefore of all of Greece. The cathedral, with a beautifully restored interior, is the centerpiece of a reverent neighborhood, with a pair of statues out front honoring great heroes of the Church.

▲Church of Agios Eleftherios

This tiny church, huddled in the shadow of the cathedral, has a delightful hodgepodge of ancient and early Christian monuments embedded in its facade. Like so many Byzantine churches, it was partly built (in the late 12th century) with fragments of earlier buildings, monuments, and even tombstones.

Syntagma Square and Nearby

These sights are covered in more detail in the 📖 Athens City Walk chapter and 🎧 my free audio tour.

▲Syntagma Square (Plateia Syntagmatos)

The "Times Square" of Athens is named for Greece's historic 1843 constitution, prompted by demonstrations right on this square. A major transit hub, the square is watched over by Neoclassical masterpieces such as the Hotel Grande Bretagne and the Parliament building.

Parliament

The former palace of King Otto is now a house of democracy. In front, colorfully costumed evzone guards stand at attention at the Tomb of the Unknown Soldier and periodically do a ceremonial changing of the guard to the delight of tourists.

▲Ermou Street

This pedestrianized thoroughfare, connecting Syntagma Square with Monastiraki (and on to Thissio and Keramikos Cemetery), is packed with international chain stores. It's enjoyable for people-watching and is refreshingly traffic-free in an otherwise congested area.

SOUTHEAST OF SYNTAGMA

For locations of these sights, see the "Athens" map on page 4.

National Garden

Extending south from the parliament, the National Garden is a wonderfully cool retreat from the traffic-clogged streets of central Athens. Covering an area of around 40 acres, it was planted in 1839 as the palace garden, created for the pleasure of Queen Amalia. Opened to the public in 1923, the garden has many pleasant paths, a café, WCs, scattered picturesque ancient columns, a playground, and several zoo-type exhibits of animals.

▸ *Free, open daily from dawn to dusk.*

Zappeion

At the southern end of the National Garden stands the grand mansion called the Zappeion, surrounded by formal gardens of its own. To most Athenians, the Zappeion is best known as the site of the Aigli Village outdoor cinema in summer (behind the building, on the right as you face the colonnaded main entry; for details, see the Activities chapter). But the building is more than just a backdrop. During Ottoman rule, much of the Greek elite, intelligentsia, and aristocracy fled the country. They returned after independence and built grand mansions such as this. Finished in 1888, it was designed by the Danish architect Theophilus Hansen, who was known (along with his brother Christian) for his Neoclassical designs. The financing was provided by the Zappas brothers, Evangelos and Konstantinos, two of the prime movers in the campaign to revive the Olympic Games. This mansion housed the International Olympic Committee during the first modern Olympics in 1896 and served as a media center during the 2004 Olympics. Today the Zappeion is a conference and exhibition center.

▶ *Gardens free and always open, building only open during exhibitions for a fee; Vasilissis Amalias, Metro: Akropoli or Evangelismos.*

▲Panathenaic (a.k.a. "Olympic") Stadium

Built in the fourth century BC to host the Panathenaic Games, the Panathenaic Stadium is your chance to see an intact ancient stadium. It's sometimes referred to as the Roman Stadium, because it was rebuilt by the great Roman benefactor Herodes Atticus in the second century AD, using the same prized Pentelic marble that was used in the Parthenon. This magnificent material gives the place its most popular name: Kalimarmaro ("Beautiful Marble") Stadium.

The stadium was restored to its Roman condition in preparation for the first modern Olympics in 1896. It saw Olympic action again in 2004 when it provided a grand finish for the marathon and a wonderful backdrop for the Paralympics opening ceremony. Today, it's occasionally used for ceremonies and concerts. In ancient times, around 50,000 spectators filled the stadium; today, it seats about 45,000 people.

Take a lap around the track, pose on the podium, and visit the modest permanent exhibit, showcasing various memorabilia commemorating the modern games.

▶ *€5, includes good audioguide; daily 8:00-19:00, Nov-Feb until 17:00; southeast of the Zappeion off Vasileos Konstantinou, Metro: Akropoli or Evangelismos, tel. 210-752-2985, www.panathenaicstadium.gr.*

NORTH OF THE CENTER

For locations of these sights, see the "Athens" map on page 4.

▲▲Psyrri

This funky district, just north of the Ancient Agora, offers a real-world alternative to the tourist-clogged, artificial-feeling Plaka. While parts are outwardly grungy and run-down, Psyrri has blossomed with a fun range of eateries, cafés, and clubs, with everything from dives to exclusive dance halls to crank-'em-out chain restaurants (for recommendations on where to eat, see the Eating chapter).

The white-marbled Panathenaic Stadium   Central Market—where the locals shop

▲Central Market
Take a vibrant, fragrant stroll through the modern-day version of the Ancient Agora. It's a living, breathing, and smelly barrage on all the senses. You'll see dripping-fresh meat, livestock in all stages of dismemberment, still-wriggling fish, exotic nuts, and sticky figs. It may not be Europe's most charming market, but it offers a lively contrast to Athens' ancient sites. The entire market square is a delight to explore, with a dizzying variety of great street food and a carnival of people-watching.

▶ *Mon-Sat 7:00-15:00, closed Sun, on Athinas between Sofokleous and Evripidou, between Metro stops Omonia and Monastiraki.*

▲▲▲National Archaeological Museum
This museum is the single best place on earth to see ancient Greek artifacts from 7000 BC to AD 500.

    📖 See the National Archaeological Museum Tour chapter or 🎧 download my free audio tour.

THE KOLONAKI MUSEUM STRIP, EAST OF SYNTAGMA SQUARE

For locations of these sights, see the "Athens" map on page 4.

▲▲Benaki Museum of Greek History and Culture
This exquisite collection takes you on a fascinating walk through the ages. And, as it's housed in a gorgeous Neoclassical mansion, it gives a peek at how Athens' upper crust lived back in the 19th century. The mind-boggling array of artifacts—which could keep a museum lover

busy for hours—is crammed into 36 galleries on four floors, covering seemingly every era of history: antiquity, Byzantine, Ottoman, and modern. Each item is labeled in English, and it's all air-conditioned.

First you'll see fine painted vases, gold wreaths of myrtle leaves worn on heads 2,300 years ago, and evocative Byzantine icons and jewelry. Look for Byzantine icon art, including two pieces by Domenikos Theotokopoulos before he became El Greco (in a glass case in the center of Room 12).

Upstairs, the first floor picks up where most Athens museums leave off: the period of Ottoman and Venetian occupation. Here you'll find traditional costumes, furniture, household items, farm implements, musical instruments, and entire rooms finely carved from wood and lovingly transplanted from Northern Greece. In Rooms 22 and 23, a fascinating exhibit shows Greece through the eyes of foreign visitors, who came here in the 18th and 19th centuries (back when Athens was still a village, spiny with Ottoman minarets) to see the same ruins you're enjoying today. On the top floor, Romantic art finally brings you into the 20th century.

▶ €9; Wed-Mon 10:00-18:00 except Thu until 24:00, Sun until 16:00, closed Tue; across from back corner of National Garden at Koumbari 1, Metro: Syntagma, tel. 210-367-1000, www.benaki.gr.

▲▲Museum of Cycladic Art

This modern, cozy, enjoyable, and manageable museum shows off the largest exhibit of Cycladic art anywhere, collected by one of Greece's richest shipping families (the Goulandris clan). While you can see Cycladic art elsewhere in Athens (such as in the National Archaeological Museum), it's displayed and described most invitingly here. While the first floor is all Cycladic, there are four floors—each with a fine exhibit.

The **first floor** focuses on art from the Cycladic Islands, which surround the isle of Delos, off the coast southeast of Athens. The Aegean city-states here—predating Athens' Golden Age by 2,000 years—were populated by a mysterious people who left no written record. But they did leave behind an ample collection of fertility figurines. These come in different sizes but follow the same general pattern: skinny, standing ramrod-straight, with large alien-like heads. Some have exaggerated breasts and hips, giving them a violin-like silhouette. Others (likely symbolizing pregnancy) appear to be clutching their midsections with both arms. These items give an insight into the matriarchal cultures of the Cycladic Islands.

While that first floor is the headliner, don't miss three more floors of exhibits upstairs: ancient Greek art, Cypriot antiquities, and scenes from daily life in antiquity. The highlight—for some, even better than the Cycladic art itself—is the engrossing **top-floor exhibit** that explains ancient Greek lifestyles. Artifacts, engaging illustrations, and vivid English descriptions resurrect a fun cross-section of the fascinating and sometimes bizarre practices of the ancients: weddings, athletics, agora culture, warfare, and various female- and male-only activities.

▶ *€7, half-price on Mon and off-season; Wed-Mon 10:00-17:00 except Thu until 20:00, Sun from 11:00, closed Tue; Neophytou Douka 4, Metro: Evangelismos, tel. 210-722-8321, www.cycladic.gr.*

▲▲Byzantine and Christian Museum

This excellent museum displays key artifacts from the Byzantine era—the 1,000-year period (c. AD 330-1453) that came after Greece's ancient glory days. While the rest of Europe fell into the Dark Ages, Byzantium shone brightly, with Athens as a key part. And, as the empire's dominant language and culture were Greek, today's Greeks proudly consider the Byzantine Empire "theirs." In this museum, you'll see bits of 2,000-year-old rubble, medieval tableware, exquisite gold religious objects, and lots and lots of icons.

The museum's layout can be confusing, as the "rooms" flow into each other without clear divisions. Use the information below to get

The fine Byzantine and Christian Museum...

...showing off 1,000 years of glory

a thematic overview, then browse freely among the many interesting and beautiful objects.

Three maps in the **entryway** show snapshots of the Byzantine world: First (AD 337-565), it was huge, when it was synonymous with the Roman Empire. When Rome fell, its eastern half (called Byzantium) carried on as the most enlightened force in Europe (1056). By the end of the Byzantine era (1453), the empire was smaller still, with only two major cities—Constantinople and Athens.

The statuettes and reliefs in **Room I.1** show how pagan Rome became Christian Byzantium. A pagan shepherd became the Bible's "Good Shepherd;" the myth of Orpheus with his lyre symbolized the goodness of Creation; and ancient philosophers became wise Jesus.

Continue down the first set of stairs into **Room I.2.** In secular life, ancient Roman knowhow continued on into medieval times, with high-quality Byzantine jewelry, ceramics, glassware, coins, and good luck charms (*eulogiai*). Descend the next steps to **Room I.3** to find column fragments and a mosaic floor (depicting animals and ancient laurel wreaths) that suggest how the same structural elements of the Roman basilica (or assembly hall) evolved into the Christian basilica (or church). In **Room I.4,** stone fragments like these, from ruined ancient temples, were recycled to build Christian churches, while the Parthenon was repurposed as Athens' cathedral.

With the fall of Rome, the Byzantine world (as the museum plaque says) entered an "Age of Crisis," marked by invading barbarians sweeping across Europe. The few broken stone fragments displayed in **Room II.2** attest to how little art survived.

While Western Europe was in shambles, the Byzantine world was held together by strong emperors and the "eastern pope," the Orthodox patriarch. See their symbols of authority in **Room II.1:** chain-mail armor, the long scroll of a patriarchal decree, coins with imperial insignia, and signet rings.

In **Rooms II.3 and II.4,** you'll see how the Christian faith in Eastern Europe was evolving into what we now call Orthodox, with its distinct imagery and rituals. On display are uniquely Orthodox painted icons: of Mary-and-the-Babe, Jesus-as-Pantocrator ("All Powerful"), and a double-sided icon that was paraded atop a pole during services.

The room to the right **(II.5)** shows how Athenian churches (such as the Church of Kapnikarea) developed their own unique style, featuring wall frescoes like these, and topped with a Pantocrator in the dome (like the one at the end of the room).

Breeze quickly through Rooms **II.6-9,** with artifacts from Byzantium's declining years (c. 1200-1400). By the 13th century, Venetian merchants (the "Latins") were asserting their power in the Byzantine trading empire. Still, the cities of Constantinople and Athens remained more civilized than the medieval west, as attested by the collection of finely worked carved reliefs and ceramics.

Browse **Room IV.1-2** to its far left end. The paintings are bigger, brighter, and more realistic, with hints of 3-D background. Unlike the stiff, flat icons of an earlier age, now saints pose with the relaxed gravitas of ancient statues. It's clear that, with the arrival of the Venetians, there was cross-pollination between Byzantine icon-makers (in Crete, Ionia, and Athens) and the budding Renaissance painters of Italy.

Then, overnight, the Byzantine Empire came to an end. Make a U-turn to the right at the far end of the hall, into Room **IV.3.** In 1453, the Ottoman Turks conquered Constantinople, and the Byzantine Empire was suddenly Muslim. In Greece, Christians (called *Romioi*) carried on their faith under Islamic rule (1453-1832). They developed the rich worship regalia still used today—icons, miters, silver vessels, and gold-embroidered vestments.

In the far left corner, step into the darkened **Room IV.4.** The printed book helped shape a common Greek identity ("the New Hellenism"), spurring the desire to be free of Ottoman rule and create the modern democratic nation of Greece.

Back upstairs, the final displays in **Room IV.5** bring Byzantium up to modern times, mainly in its legacy to religious art. The flat simplified techniques of Byzantine art have even influenced modern abstract painters—a timeless style that's, well, iconic.

▶ *€8; daily 8:00-20:00 except Tue from 12:30; excellent café/restaurant, Vasilissis Sofias 22, Metro: Evangelismos, tel. 213-213-9517, www. byzantinemuseum.gr.*

DAY TRIPS FROM ATHENS

The following destinations are doable in a day from Athens. But they'll be much more satisfying with an overnight or as part of a longer Greece itinerary. For more information, see my *Rick Steves Greece: Athens & the Peloponnese* guidebook.

▲▲▲Hydra

In under two hours, you can sail to this glamorous getaway, combining practical convenience with idyllic Greek island ambience. While Hydra (EE-drah) can be done as a long day trip from Athens, it's better to spend two nights (or more) so you can really relax.

One of the island's greatest attractions is its total absence of cars and motorbikes. Sure-footed donkeys—laden with everything from sandbags and bathtubs to bottled water—climb stepped lanes. The island's main town, also called Hydra, is one of Greece's prettiest. Its busy but quaint harbor—bobbing with rustic fishing boats and luxury yachts—is surrounded by a ring of rocky hills and whitewashed homes. From the harbor, zippy water taxis whisk you to isolated beaches and tavernas.

▶ ***Getting There:*** *To reach Hydra, take a Hellenic Seaways high-speed hydrofoil ("Flying Dolphin") or catamaran ("Flying Cat"). Boats leave from the port of Piraeus (near central Athens—see page 188) frequently (6-8/day June-Sept, 4/day Oct-May, 1.5-2 hours; for tickets, visit a travel agency, call, or go online—tel. 210-419-9000, www.hellenicseaways.gr). Note that it's wise to book well in advance, especially for summer weekends, and that weather conditions can cause cancellations.*

Hydra—Greek-isle ambience two hours away

On Hydra, donkeys do the heavy lifting.

Delphi's photogenic Sanctuary of Athena

▲▲Delphi

Outside of Athens, this is the most spectacular of Greece's ancient sites. Long ago, Delphi was the home of a prophetess known as the oracle (a.k.a. the Pythia), the mouthpiece of Apollo on earth. Pilgrims came from far and wide to seek her advice on everything from affairs of state to wars to matrimonial problems. Delphi's fame grew, and its religious festivals blossomed into the Pythian Games, an athletic contest that was second only to the Olympics. Today visitors can see the archaeological site, containing the ruins of the Sanctuary of Apollo, and the great Archaeological Museum, where statues and treasures found on the site help bring the ruins to life.

▶ *€12 to enter both the site and museum (€6 off-season); 18 and under free—be prepared to show ID; both the site and museum are open daily 8:00-20:00 in summer (generally April-Oct); in winter, both are open daily 9:00-15:00. Confirm opening times in advance—tel. 22650-82312, http://odysseus.culture.gr.*

    Getting There: *Buses between Delphi and Athens depart every few hours (4-5/day, 3 hours). It's a 10-minute walk to the archaeological site from the bus stop (smart to buy return ticket as soon as you arrive, because buses can fill up). Or join a package tour from Athens, which* *includes transportation, a guided tour, and lunch (see the Activities chapter).*

The Peloponnese

▲▲▲Nafplio

Once the capital of a newly independent Greece (19th century), this historically important town is small, cozy, and strollable. While the town's glory days have faded, Nafplio retains a certain genteel panache. Walk the narrow and atmospheric back streets, lined with elegant Venetian houses and Neoclassical mansions. Dip into the fine archaeological museum, featuring relics from prehistoric Greece and the Mycenaean civilization. Or hike up to Palamidi Fortress, one of three Venetian-built castles guarding the harbor (all wonderfully floodlit at night). The best-preserved castle of its kind in Greece, Palamidi towers over the Old Town, protected to the west by steep cliffs that plunge 650 feet to the sea.

▶ **Getting There:** *It's an easy 2.5-hour drive or bus ride from Athens (buses run nearly hourly, www.ktelargolida.gr).*

▲Epidavros

Nestled in a leafy valley some 20 miles east of Nafplio, Epidavros was once the most famous healing center in the ancient Greek world. Since pilgrims prayed to Asklepios, the god of medicine, for health, a sanctuary was needed, with a temple, altars, and statues to the gods. The sanctuary reached the height of its popularity in the fourth and third centuries BC, when it boasted medical facilities, housing for the sick, mineral baths, a stadium for athletic competitions, and a theater.

Nafplio—history, atmosphere, and seafood

Test the acoustics at Epidavros' theater.

Mycenae's Treasury of Atreus: royal burial place

These days the famous theater is Epidavros' star attraction. Built into the side of a tree-covered hill, it's the finest and best-preserved of all of Greece's ancient theaters—and that's saying something in a country with 132 of them.

▶ *€12 (€6 off-season) includes theater, museum, and archaeological site; daily April-Oct 8:00-20:00, off-season 8:00-15:00, check times locally; tel. 27350-22009, http://odysseus.culture.gr.*

   Getting There: *From Nafplio, it's a 30-minute drive or 45-minute bus ride (Mon-Sat 3-4/day). From Athens, buses head to Nafplio, then continue on to Epidavros (2-3/day, 2.5 hours, might require a transfer in Nafplio, www.ktelargolida.gr).*

▲Mycenae

This fortress city atop a hill was the hub of a mighty civilization that dominated the Greek world between 1600 and 1200 BC, a thousand years before Athens' Golden Age. Today, a visit to Mycenae is a trip back into prehistory to see some of the oldest remains of a complex civilization in Europe. The three main attractions are the archaeological ruins, consisting of the hilltop walled city with its grand Lion Gate entrance; a museum housing artifacts that were found here; and the impressive Treasury of Atreus—a huge domed tomb where Mycenae's royalty were buried.

▶ *€12 (€6 off-season) includes archaeological site, museum, and Treasury of Atreus; roughly daily 8:00-20:00, closes an hour or two earlier in fall; Nov-April daily until 15:00; hours can change without notice—ask your hotel or call ahead; tel. 27510-76802 or 27520-27502, http://odysseus.culture.gr.*

Getting There: *It's 30 minutes by car or 45 minutes by bus from Nafplio (Mon-Sat 2-3/day, confirm that your bus goes to the archaeological site—other buses take you only as far as Fichti, two miles away; www.ktelargolidas.gr).*

Activities

Athens is a thriving city, and you'll never run out of things to do here. This chapter offers suggestions for tours (including bus, walking, and food tours that allow you to sample Greece's famously delicious cuisine), along with ideas for shopping and evening entertainment.

Athenians know how to have a good time, especially after hours. From folk performances to outdoor movies, rooftop cocktails to simply strolling around, you'll find many options for a memorable evening. The city is most inviting from May through October (aside from miserably hot August), when al fresco activities such as outdoor cinema, festivals, folk-dancing shows, and sidewalk cafés and bars are in full swing.

TOURS

🎧 To sightsee on your own, download my free audio tours that illuminate some of Athens' top sights and neighborhoods (see sidebar on page 11).

Bus Tours

Various companies offer half-day, bus-plus-walking tours of Athens that include a guided visit to the Acropolis (about €60). Longer tours also include a guided tour of the Acropolis Museum (€70-80). Some companies also offer a night city tour that finishes with dinner and folk dancing at a taverna (€66) as well as longer excursions outside the city. The most established operations include the well-regarded **Hop In** (tel. 210-428-5500, www.hopin.com), **CHAT Tours** (tel. 210-323-0827, www.chat-tours.com), **Key Tours** (tel. 210-923-3166, www.keytours.gr), and **G.O. Tours** (tel. 210-921-9555, www.gotours.com.gr).

Some of these companies also offer day-long tours to Delphi and to Mycenae, Nafplio, and Epidavros (either tour around €100 with lunch, €85 without). **Tune In Tours** offers day trips, as well as airport transfers and customized private tours of Athens (reasonable rates, mobile 697-320-1213, www.tuneintours.com).

Hop-On, Hop-Off Bus Tours

Several hop-on, hop-off bus-tour companies offer 1.5-hour loops and 24-hour tickets for €16-25, including **CitySightseeing Athens** (red buses, www.citysightseeing.gr), **Athens Open Tour** (yellow buses, www.athensopentour.com), and the cheaper **Open Top Bus** (blue buses, www.sightsofathens.gr). The main stop is on Syntagma Square, though you can hop on and buy your ticket at any stop—look for signs around town. I'd use this only if I wanted an overview of the city or had extra time to get to the outlying sights.

Walking Tours

Athens Walking Tours offers several walks of the city and major sights (€29-59, 1.5-5.5 hours) as well as food and wine tours (tel. 210-884-7269, mobile 694-585-9662, www.athenswalkingtours.gr).

Context Athens' "intellectual by design" walking tours are geared for serious learners and led by "docents" rather than by guides (US tel. 800-691-8328, www.contexttravel.com/city/athens).

ACTIVITIES

Alternative Athens delves into the Greek capital's contemporary side. They run excellent food tours, as well as walks focusing on street art, Greek designers, Athens' neighborhoods, and Greek mythology (tel. 211-012-6544, mobile 694-840-5242, www.alternative athens.com).

Food Tours

A good way to experience Greek culture is through its cuisine. With a good food tour, you'll learn a lot about Greek history and culture, plus you'll get to sample classic dishes. **Alternative Athens** offers a 3.5-hour tour and home-cooked meal experiences (tel. 211-012-6544, mobile 69484-05242, www.alternativeathens.com). **Culinary Backstreets'** longer tours are for people who love to eat. They offer several tours (each 5.5 hours), the groups are smaller, and you'll eat more unique food $135/person; 2-7 people, www.culinarybackstreets. com).

Local Guides

A good private guide can bring Athens' sights to life. I've enjoyed working with each of these guides: **Faye Georgiou** (mobile 697-768-5503, fayegeorgiou@yahoo.gr); **Dora Mavrommati** (mobile 694-689-9300, mavrom.dor@gmail.com); **Apostolos Douras** (mobile 697-854-4912, adouras@gmail.com); **Danae Kousouri** (mobile 697-353-3219, danae kousouri@gmail.com); **Niki Vlachou** (mobile 697-242-6085, niki@ olympic.gr); **Angelos Kokkaliaris** (mobile 697-412-7127, www.athens walkingguide.com); **Anastasia Gaitanou** (mobile 694-446-3109, anastasia2570@yahoo.com); and **Effie Perperi** (mobile 697-739-6659, effieperperi@gmail.com).

SHOPPING

Most shops catering to tourists are open long hours daily (souvenir stores in the Plaka can be open past midnight). Afternoon breaks are common, and some places close early a few nights a week.

Where to Shop

Shopping Streets: The main streets of the Plaka—especially **Adrianou** and **Pandrossou**—are crammed with crass tourist-trap shops selling kitschy trinkets. Competition is fierce, so there's room to bargain, especially if you're buying several items. If you're determined to shop here, look for typical Grecian clothing, sandals, or cosmetics.

For midrange shopping at mostly international chain stores, stroll the pedestrianized **Ermou street** between Syntagma Square and Monastiraki. You'll find more local flavor at Greek shops such as **Kem** (handbags; Kornarou 1, just off Ermou), **Heroes** (unique Greek-themed jewelry and accessories, handmade by Athens native Eugenia Kokkala-Mela; Aiolou 9, just off Ermou), and the clothing stores **Regalinas** (Ermou 37) and **Bill Cost** (Ermou 14). Many locals prefer the more authentic shops on the streets just to the north, such as **Perikleous, Lekka,** and **Kolokotroni.**

Monastiraki Flea Market: This famous flea market stretches west of Monastiraki Square, along Ifestou street and its side streets. You'll see plenty of souvenir shops, but the heart of the market is Avissinias Square, filled with antique shops. There's something going on every day, but the market is best and most crowded on Sundays, when store owners lay out the stuff they've been scouting for all week. If buying here, make sure to bargain (Sun flea market open 8:00-15:00, packed with locals by 10:00, Metro: Monastiraki or Thissio).

Department Store: The largest department store in Athens is **Attica,** which has a cafeteria on the top floor but no views (Mon-Fri 10:00-21:00, Sat until 20:00, closed Sun, near Syntagma Square at 9 Panepistimiou, tel. 211-180-2600).

What to Buy

Higher-End Souvenirs: Check out these shops for a thoughtfully curated selection of artsy souvenirs. **Forget Me Not** sells ceramics,

Kitschy trinkets on Adrianou street...

...and international chains on Ermou street

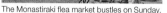

The Monastiraki flea market bustles on Sunday. Melissinos Art, custom-made sandals since 1920

housewares, fun T-shirts, and locally produced clothing and beach-wear (Adrianou 100, tel. 210-325-3740, www.forgetmenotathens.gr). **Thíkı** has totes, T-shirts, pillowcases, and stationery featuring famous Greek quotes and evil-eye designs (Adrianou 120, tel. 210-323-5234, www.thikigreece.com). The **Museum of Greek Folk Art**'s gift shop also offers a range of tasteful items inspired by their museum collection (Thespidos 4, just off Adrianou).

Jewelry: Serious buyers say that Athens is the best place in Greece to purchase jewelry, particularly at the **shops along Adrianou.** The choices are much better, and—if you know how to haggle—so are the prices. The best advice is to take your time, and don't be afraid to walk away. The sales staff gets paid on commission, and they hate to lose a potential customer.

For something a bit more specialized (with high prices), visit **Byzantino,** which made the jewelry worn by Greek dancers in the closing ceremonies of the 2000 Sydney Olympics. They create pricey handmade replicas of museum pieces, along with some original designs (daily 10:00-21:00, Adrianou 120, tel. 210-324-6605, www.byzantino.com, run by Kosta).

Olympico creates their own modern pieces in the Greek style, along with museum copies. They also sell pieces made by artisans from all over Greece (daily 11:00-22:00, shorter hours off-season, Adrianou 122, tel. 210-324-8697, www.olympicojewlery.com, George).

The gift shop at the **Benaki Museum of Greek History and Culture** is also popular for its jewelry.

Handmade Sandals: The best place to buy real leather sandals is **Melissinos Art**. The famous Pantelis Melissinos, who's also a poet, painter, and playwright, is the third generation in his craft. This shop

Worry Beads

As you travel through Greece, you may notice Greek men fidgeting with their worry beads. Greeks use these beaded strings to soothe themselves and get focused—especially during hard times. Loosely based on prayer beads, but today a secular hobby, worry beads make for a fun Greek souvenir. You'll see them sold all over central Athens.

The beads are made from a variety of materials. The basic tourist version is a cheap "starter set" made from synthetic materials, similar to marbles. You'll pay more for organic materials, which are considered more pleasant to touch: precious stones, bones, horn, wood, coral, mother-of-pearl, seeds, and more. The most prized worry beads are made of amber. Most valuable are the hand-cut amber beads, which are very soft and fragile; machine-cut amber is processed to be stronger.

When buying, try several different strings to find one that fits well in your hand; tune in to the smoothness of the beads and the sound they make when clacking together.

has been an Athens landmark since 1920. In the windows, you'll see photos of celebrities who have worn Melissinos sandals over the decades, from Jackie O. to John Lennon. Inside, you'll find an assortment of styles in basic shades of tan for about €40-50 per pair. They can also customize a pair for you (daily 10:00-18:00, two blocks down Athanasiou Diakou from the Akropoli metro station in Makrigianni, Tzireon 16, tel. 210-321-9247, www.melissinos-art.com).

For a more contemporary, fashion-forward pair of sandals, try the **Ancient Greek Sandals** boutique near Syntagma Square (Mon-Sat 10:00-20:00, closed Sun; Kolokotroni 1, tel. 210-323-0938, www.ancient-greek-sandals.com).

Religious Items: Icons and other Greek Orthodox objects can make good souvenirs. For the best selection, visit the shops near the cathedral, along Agia Filotheis street (most are closed Sat-Sun).

Specialty Foods

All over Athens specialty food stores sell locally produced goods, such as olive oil, wine and liqueurs, and sweets like boxed baklava, *halva* (a confection usually made from sesame paste), *loukoumi* (a.k.a. Greek delight), and jars of "spoon sweets" (jam-like spreads).

The best place to shop for these is where the locals do—near the **Central Market.** Specialty grocers and spice shops cluster around Athinas and Evripidou streets.

Yoleni's is a top-end, all-purpose Greek grocery store in the posh Kolonaki area, about a 10-minute walk from Syntagma Square (long hours daily, Stolonos 9, tel. 212-222-3622, www.yolenis.com). **Ergon House Deli** is stocked with artisanal products—both Greek and international—worthy of an upper-fork picnic or to bring home as souvenirs (cooking classes available, open daily 7:00-24:00, Mitropoleos 23, tel. 210-109-090, https://house.ergonfoods.com). For chocolate and other Greek goods, check out **Matsouka** (ΜΑΤΣΟΥΚΑ) and its offshoots,

Specialty foods can be sampled in and around the Central Market.

around the corner from Syntagma Square (main branch at Karageorgi Servias 10, other shops nearby, daily 8:00-23:00).

Also near Syntagma Square, **Mastiha Shop** specializes in a unique Greek treat—a sweet resin produced only by trees on a particular part of Chios island. *Mastica* has been revered since ancient times for its medicinal properties in treating stomach ailments. Drop in for some free samples (closed Sun, a block above Syntagma Square at Panepistimiou 6, tel. 210-363-2750).

VAT and Customs

Getting a VAT Refund: If you purchase more than €50 worth of goods at a single store, you may be eligible to get a refund of about 24 percent Value-Added Tax (VAT). Get more details from your merchant or see RickSteves.com/vat.

Customs for American Shoppers: You can take home $800 worth of items per person duty-free, once every 31 days. You can bring in one liter of alcohol duty-free. For details on allowable goods, customs rules, and duty rates, visit http://help.cbp.gov.

NIGHTLIFE

Athens has a constantly rotating schedule of cultural activities to suit every audience. Several lively neighborhoods have bars and clubs that stay open late, but in the heat of summer, some clubs close down to relocate to outdoor venues on the coast. A number of tavernas feature live music and dancing locals year-round, providing a wonderful setting for a late dinner.

Festivals

Athens' biggest party is the **Athens & Epidavros Festival,** held every June and July. The festival's highlights are its world-class performances of dance, music, and theater at the ancient Odeon of Herodes Atticus, nestled spectacularly below the floodlit Acropolis. Tickets go on sale from late April to early May. You can buy them online, over the phone, and at the festival box office (closed Sun, in the arcade at Panepistimiou 39, opposite the National Library, tel. 210-893-8112, www.greekfestival.gr).

Athens has a thriving nightlife scene.

Folk Dancing

The **Dora Stratou Theater** on Filopappos Hill is the place to go to see authentic folk dancing. The theater company—the best in Greece—was originally formed to record and preserve the country's many traditional dances. Performances rotate, but their repertoire includes such favorites as the graceful *kalamatianos* circle dance, the *syrtaki* (famously immortalized by Anthony Quinn in *Zorba the Greek*), and the dramatic solo *zimbetikos* (€15, 1.5-hour performances run June-late Sept, generally Wed-Fri at 21:30, Sat-Sun at 20:30, no shows Mon-Tue; take Metro to Petralona, then walk 10 minutes; morning tel. 210-324-4395, evening tel. 210-921-4650, www.grdance.org).

Outdoor Cinema

Athens has a wonderful tradition of outdoor movies. Screenings take place most nights in summer (around €10, roughly June-Sept, sometimes in May and Oct depending on weather; shows start around 20:00 or 21:00, depending on when the sun sets; many offer a second, later showing). Drinks are served at these "theaters," which are actually compact open-air courtyards with folding chairs.

Aigli Village Cinema is a cool, classic outdoor theater in the National Garden (at the Zappeion), playing the latest blockbusters with a great sound system (tel. 210-336-9369, www.aeglizappiou.gr). **Cine Paris,** in the Plaka, shows movies on the roof with Acropolis views (overlooking Filomousou Square at Kidathineon 22, tel. 210-322-2071, www.cineparis.gr). **Cine Theseion,** along the Apostolou Pavlou pedestrian drag in the Thissio neighborhood, enjoys grand floodlit Acropolis views from some of its seats—one of the reasons it was voted the "best outdoor cinema in the world" (Apostolou Pavlou 7, tel. 210-347-0980 or 210-342-0864, www.cine-thisio.gr).

Strolling After Dark

A peaceful pedestrian lane circles the Acropolis, providing locals and visitors alike a delightful place for an evening stroll. This promenade is what I call the "Acropolis Loop" (consisting of Dionysiou Areopagitou to the south and Apostolou Pavlou to the west; for details, see page 134).

The promenade cuts through the Thissio district, just beyond the Agora, where the tables and couches of clubs and cocktail bars clog the pedestrian lanes under the Acropolis. More upscale than the Plaka,

Evening strolls come with views of a floodlit Acropolis.

Thissio gives you an easy escape from the tired tourism of that zone. Thissio is basically composed of three or four streets running into Apostolou Pavlou (part of the "Acropolis Loop"). Iraklidon street is a tight lane with people socializing at café tables squeezed under trees. Akamantos street, while still colorful, is a bit more sedate. As the sun sets and the floodlit temples of the Acropolis ornament the horizon, you understand why this quiet and breezy corner is such a hit with locals enjoying an evening out.

Come here just to stroll through a fine café scene, enjoy a drink and some great people-watching, or see a movie under the stars (at Cine Theseion, listed earlier).

Bars, Cafés, And Late-Night Spots

Athens abounds with bars and cafés serving drinks in lively and atmospheric settings (including on rooftops boasting grand views). Note that although bars are supposed to be nonsmoking, many places don't adhere to this rule.

Plaka: Although the Plaka is jammed full of tourists and few locals, it couldn't be more central or user-friendly, with live traditional music spilling out of seemingly every other taverna. One pleasant area to explore is the stepped lane called **Mnisikleous.** Or try **Brettos,**

Brettos: Athens' oldest distillery

Lively Iroon Square in Psyrri

the oldest distillery in Athens, dating from 1909 (just off Adrianou at Kydathineon 41, tel. 210-323-2100).

For drinks, I also enjoy the following wine bars (which also serve good food): **By the Glass** (near the National Garden at Souri 3, inside the InnAthens hotel, tel. 210-323-2560) and **Heteroclito** (near the cathedral, Fokionos 2 at corner with Petraki, tel. 201-323-9406).

Monastiraki: Right on Monastiraki Square, several rooftop bars offer some of the best views of the city (see "Rooftop Bars," later). Nearby, the **TAF Art Foundation** is a hidden garden café and bar in one of Athens' oldest houses (Normanou 5, tel. 210-323-8757).

Adrianou Street: This street just north of the Agora has a line of inviting restaurants and cafés with outdoor seating—some with spectacular Acropolis views and all good for a drink.

Psyrri: The center of this seedy-chic district is Iroon Square, with several cute bar/cafés spilling into the square under a jolly mural. Nearby Lepeniotou and Esopou streets are fun for their creatively decorated places. **Juan Rodriguez,** a block off Athinas, is a noisy Art Deco/Roaring Twenties-style bar packed with locals—it's often standing room only (Pallados 3, tel. 210-322-4496).

Near St. Irene Square: The square surrounding the Church of St. Irene, across busy Athinas street just east of Psyrri, offers one of the most delightful wine-and-coffee scenes in the center.

Around Kolokotroni and Praxitelous Streets: These lively streets, north of Syntagma and Monastiraki, offer a mix of open-air courtyards, high-end cocktails, contemporary charm, and classic dive-bar atmosphere. Try **Noel** (on a lively square lined with outdoor tables, Kolokotroni 59, tel. 211-215-9534); **Booze Bar** (time-warp, '90s-era dive, Kolokotroni 57, tel. 211-405-3733); or **Baba au Rum** (seriously good cocktails, Klitiou 6, tel. 211-710-9140). **The Clumsies** tops all the "best of" lists—its creatively crafted cocktails are works of liquid art (Praxitelous 30, tel. 210-323-2682).

Rooftop Bars

Plaka/Syntagma: For a great view and overpriced cocktails, visit the recommended rooftop restaurant and bar of the **Hotel Grande Bretagne,** across the street from Syntagma Square. There are also several rooftop bars at hotels near the Acropolis Museum, including the Sense Restaurant, on top of the **Athenswas Hotel** (5 Dionysiou Areopagitou), and the Point α Bar at the **Herodion Hotel** (4 Rovertou Galli).

Monastiraki: The rooftop of the **A for Athens** hotel is popular with both locals and tourists who come to gawk at its views. If this place is too crowded, try the **360 Cocktail Bar** on the same square (but with less impressive panoramas).

Next door to the Monastiraki flea market, **Couleur Locale** has a getaway rooftop bar and third-floor terrace (also a restaurant, Normanou 3, tel. 216-700-4917).

Thissio: If strolling the pedestrian promenade through Thissio, consider a stop at the **Thissio View** restaurant and bar (Apostolou Pavlou 25).

Psyrri: Overlooking the Church of St. Irene, the rooftop bar at **Monk** is good for both food and drink (Karori 4).

Sleeping

Athens' central core (the Plaka, Syntagma, and Monastiraki) has some fancy business-class hotels, while small, inexpensive guesthouses are relatively scarce and overbooked. For more options, expand your search. The lively Psyrri district is worth considering—it's close to the center, stuffed with enticing food options, and near major sights. I've also found a few gems in Makrigianni and Koukaki, behind the Acropolis and a short walk from the Plaka action.

I like places that are clean, central, relatively quiet at night, reasonably priced, friendly, small enough to have a hands-on owner or manager, and run with a respect for Greek traditions. The accommodations listed here cluster around the €95-150 range but include everything from €25 bunks to deluxe €350 doubles.

Athens Hotels

In general, temper your expectations. Athenian buildings are often cheaply constructed, with well-worn public spaces and temperamental plumbing and elevators. A welcoming front-desk staff can help compensate, but be ready for hiccups. Any hotel charging less than about €100 may include a few quirks. Spending just €20-30 extra is enough to buy you a much higher degree of comfort. If you're even a little high maintenance (be honest), consider splurging here. If you want an Acropolis-view room, you'll usually pay a higher rate. Budget travelers: Don't be sucked in by *very* cheap, too-good-to-be-true deals (most of those hotels are located in sleazy districts around Omonia Square, or down in the coastal suburbs of Glyfada and Voula).

Athens is a noisy city, and Athenians like to stay out late. This, combined with an epidemic of flimsy construction and the abundance of heavy traffic on city streets, can make things challenging for light sleepers. I've tried to recommend places in quieter areas, but finding a peaceful corner isn't always possible (be ready to use earplugs).

All over Greece, including Athens, most bathrooms have ancient plumbing that clogs easily. You may see signs requesting that you discard toilet paper in the bathroom wastebasket. This may seem unusual, but it keeps the sewer system working and prevents you from getting cozy with your hotel janitor.

Making Reservations

Reserve your rooms as soon as you've pinned down your travel dates. Book your room directly via email, phone, or through the hotel's official website (not a booking website). The hotelier wants to know:

- Type(s) of rooms you want and size of your party
- Number of nights you'll stay
- Arrival and departure dates, written European-style as day/month/year (for example, 18/06/22 or 18 June 2022)
- Special requests (en suite bathroom, cheapest room, twin beds vs. double bed, quiet room)
- Applicable discounts (such as a Rick Steves discount, cash discount, or promotional rate)

Most places will request a credit-card number to hold your room. If the hotel's website doesn't have a secure form where you can enter the number directly, share that info via a phone call.

Sleep Code

Dollar signs reflect the average price of a standard double room with breakfast in high season.

$$$$	**Splurge:** Most rooms over €150
$$$	**Pricier:** €110-150
$$	**Moderate:** €70-110
$	**Budget:** €50-70
¢	**Backpacker:** Under €50
RS%	**Rick Steves discount**

Unless otherwise noted, credit cards are accepted, hotel staff speak basic English, and free Wi-Fi is available.

If you must cancel, it's courteous—and smart—to do so with as much notice as possible, especially for smaller family-run places. Cancellation policies can be strict; read the fine print before you book. Always call or email to reconfirm your room reservation a few days in advance. For *dhomatia* (privately rented rooms) or very small hotels, I call again on my day of arrival to tell my host what time to expect me (especially important if arriving late—after 17:00).

Budget Tips

Comparison-shop by checking prices at several hotels (on each hotel's own website, on a booking site, or by email). For the best deal, *book directly with the hotel.* Ask for a discount if paying in cash. If the listing includes **RS%,** request a Rick Steves discount.

For some travelers, short-term, Airbnb-type rentals can be a good alternative; search for places in my recommended hotel neighborhoods. You can often find a well-equipped, spacious, centrally located apartment for less than the cost of a midrange hotel room. Given the hit-or-miss quality of Athenian hotels, a carefully chosen apartment can be an excellent value.

Websites such as Airbnb, FlipKey, Booking.com, and the HomeAway family of sites (HomeAway, VRBO, and VacationRentals) let you browse a wide range of properties. Alternatively, rental agencies such as InterhomeUSA.com and RentaVilla.com, which list more carefully selected accommodations that might cost more, can provide more personalized service.

PLAKA, SYNTAGMA, AND MONASTIRAKI

Central Plaka, Syntagma, and Monastiraki area, offering close proximity to the sights (you'll rarely need public transportation)

$$$$ Central Hotel 84 cookie-cutter rooms, sleek public spaces, anonymous business-class vibe, some rooms with balconies and/or views, cheaper rooms are good value, swanky rooftop terrace with bar and restaurant.

Apollonos 21, tel. 210-323-4357, www.centralhotel.gr

$$$$ InnAthens Feels urban and urbane, at the edge of the Plaka, 37 industrial-mod rooms ringing an atrium, recommended wine bar on the premises.

Souri 3, tel. 210-325-8555, www.innathens.com

$$$$ Hotel Plaka Buried on an urban street, rooftop bar/terrace, 67 modern rooms (some with Acropolis views), classy management adds nice touches, staff member on hand at breakfast to answer travel questions, RS%.

Corner of Mitropoleos and Kapnikarea, tel. 210-322-2096, www.plakahotel.gr

$$$ Hermes Hotel Professionally run, 45 rooms—some with balconies, inviting lobby, pleasant lounge, kids' activity room, rooftop patio with a peek at the Acropolis, RS%.

Apollonos 19, tel. 210-323-5514, www.hermeshotel.gr

$$$ Alice Inn Athens Four rooms filling a classic townhouse, tucked on an untouristed street, Irish-Greek owner John provides hospitality and funky charm, each room different.

Tsatsou 9, tel. 210-323-7139, www.aliceinnathens.com

$$$ The Zillers Conveniently located boutique hotel, facing the cathedral, feels posh, marble, hardwood, classic spiral staircase, friendly, six of 10 rooms have Acropolis views, roof garden restaurant and cocktail bar.

Mitropoleos 54, tel. 210-322-2278, www.thezillersathenshotel.com

$$$ Niki Athens Hotel Classy, movie-set vibe, 23 fresh and contemporary rooms, good value.

Nikis 27, tel. 210-322-0913, www.nikiathenshotel.com

$$$$ Hotel Grande Bretagne Five-star splurge, 320 sprawling and elegantly furnished rooms, considered best hotel in Greece, 19th-century elegance, breakfast extra, overlooking Syntagma Square.

Vassileos Georgiou 1, tel. 210-333-0000, www.grandebretagne.gr

$$$$ Electra Palace Athens Luxury five-star hotel, 155 rooms, quiet corner of the Plaka, pricey but plush, top-notch service, garden patio, indoor pool, Acropolis-view outdoor pool in summer.

Nikodimou 18, tel. 210-337-0000, www.electrahotels.gr

$$$ Hotel Adonis 26 retro-simple but thoughtfully managed rooms, on a quiet street, some rooms with views of the Acropolis, rooftop bar, RS%, reserve with credit card but pay in cash.

Kodrou 3, tel. 210-324-9737, www.hotel-adonis.gr

$$ Hotel Acropolis House Former wealthy lawyer's villa but feels homey, antiques scattered amid dark-wood furnishings, 23 old-fashioned rooms, many have balconies, cheaper rooms with private bathroom across the hall, reserve with credit card but pay in cash, no elevator.

Kodrou 6, tel. 210-322-2344, www.acropolishouse.gr

$$ Hotel Kimon 15 well-worn but perfectly fine rooms, handy location near the cathedral, cheaper "economy" rooms simpler and very affordable, no breakfast, no elevator, top-floor terrace with a corner that looks up at the Acropolis.

Apollonos 27, tel. 210-331-4658, www.kimonhotelathens.com

$$ Hotel Phaedra Simple but nicely located, overlooking a peaceful Plaka square, 21 plain rooms, most have balconies and views, six rooms have private bathrooms across the hall, Acropolis-view rooftop terrace, RS%, breakfast extra.

Herefondos 16, tel. 210-323-8461, www.hotelphaedra.com

¢ Student & Travellers' Inn Hostel with renovated rooms, in-house travel agency, pay laundry service, courtyard bar, kitchen.

Kidathineon 16, tel. 210-324-4808, www.studenttravellersinn.com

PSYRRI

Up-and-coming area with in-the-know restaurants, buzzing nightlife, and newer boutique hotels

$$$ St. Bjur Airy and fresh hotel, 16 decent-sized rooms, perched above busy Athinas, half a block from Monastiraki Square, good value for central location, breakfast extra.

Athinas 11, tel. 210-321-5208, www.stbjur.gr

$$$ Blend Hotel Sleek and contemporary respite, 24 varied rooms and suites, prime location along Psyrri's popular Aiolou street.

Vyssis 2, tel. 210-322-1552, www.blendhotel.gr

$$$ Athens 4 Housed in a design-forward former textile factory, oozes accessible chic, 23 uniquely styled rooms, minimalist facade and public areas.

Polyklitou 4, tel. 201-322-4524, www.athens4.com

$ Hotel Tempi Run by friendly Yiannis and Katerina, 24 spartan rooms, cramped bathrooms, rates are just right, well situated on lively St. Irene Square, some rooms with view balconies and nighttime noise, cheaper rooms with shared bathroom, no breakfast, lots of stairs, elevator for luggage only.

Aiolou 29, tel. 210-321-3175, www.tempihotel.gr

$$$ Arion Hotel Reliable option, 51 spacious business-style rooms, roof terrace between Iroon Square and the market, broken-in feeling that agrees with the neighborhood.

Agiou Dimitriou 18, tel. 210-324-0415, www.arionhotel.gr

$$ Athens Center Square Hotel 54 rooms are functional and minimalist but colorfully painted, roof garden has Acropolis views, just off Athinas street overlooking the produce market, RS%.

Aristogitonos 15, tel. 210-321-1770, www.athenscentersquarehotel.gr

MAKRIGIANNI AND KOUKAKI

Adjoining residential areas behind the Acropolis with a typically Athenian urban feel

$$$ Hotel Hera Tempting splurge, 38 plush rooms above a classy lobby, helpful service, lots of thoughtful touches, air of elegance, handy location near the Acropolis end of this neighborhood, rooftop Acropolis-view restaurant.

Falirou 9, tel. 210-923-6682, www.herahotel.gr

$$$ Athens Studios 37 good-value apartments with retro-mod decor, kitchens, sports bar and public launderette on ground floor, pay long-term luggage storage available.

Veikou 3A, tel. 210-923-5811, www.athensstudios.gr

$$ Art Gallery Hotel Comfy, well-run small hotel, 21 faded but affordable rooms, quieter part of this neighborhood, sits above the busier main thoroughfares, breakfast extra, fourth-floor bar, look for Ξενοδοχείο sign.

Erechthiou 5, tel. 210-923-8376, www.artgalleryhotel.gr

Eating

Greek food is just plain good. And Athens, the melting pot of Greece (and the Balkans), is one of the best places to experience the cuisine, thanks to a stunning variety of tasty and affordable eateries.

I've listed these restaurants by neighborhood. You probably won't be able to resist dining in the touristy Plaka at least once—it's fun, folkloric, and full of clichés (beware the tourist traps). But don't be afraid to venture elsewhere. For a trendy and youthful local scene, target Psyrri—just beyond the tourist zone. For those staying near the Acropolis Museum in Makrigianni or Koukaki, I've listed a couple of convenient options (including my two favorite elegant restaurants in all of Athens).

When in Athens

Greeks like to eat late—around 21:00 or later. Restaurants in Athens tend to stay open until midnight or even past that. Though smoking is not allowed in indoor spaces, don't be surprised to find that some restaurants and bars don't enforce the law.

To save money and time, try one of Greece's street-food specialties. Options include souvlaki (meat-on-a-skewer meal), savory pie (filled with meat, cheese, or vegetables), *koulouri* (bread rings), *loukoumades* (Greek doughnuts), and more.

Food tours are a great way to get to know Greeks, who love to cook and love to eat. For food tour recommendations, see page 155.

Restaurants

In addition to the traditional Greek restaurant *(estiatorio),* tourists and locals alike also fill **tavernas**—common, rustic neighborhood restaurants with a smaller menu, slinging Greek favorites. These tend to be cheaper, to cater to locals' budgets. You'll also see **mezedopolio,** eateries specializing in small plates/appetizers/*mezedes, and* **ouzerie,** bars that make ouzo and often sell high-quality *mezedes*—or even meals—to go along with it.

When you sit down at a restaurant, you'll likely be asked if you want a basket of (generally fresh, good) bread, often with your napkins and flatware tucked inside. You'll pay a bread and cover charge of about €0.50-1 (usually noted clearly on the menu).

Menus are usually written in both Greek and English. Many tavernas will have a display case showing what they've been cooking for the day, and it's perfectly acceptable to ask for a look and point to the dish you want. This is a good way to make some friends, sample a variety of dishes, get what you want (or at least know what you're getting), and have a truly memorable meal.

Wine, Coffee, and Sweets

There are two basic types of Greek wines—**retsina** (resin-flavored, rarely served) and **nonresinated wines.** *Retsina* wine has long been famous as the working man's Greek wine. The first glass is like drinking wood. The third glass is dangerous: It starts to taste good. If pine sap is not your cup of tea, there are plenty of nonresinated wine options. With its new generation of winemakers (many of them trained abroad), Greece is receiving more recognition for its wines. The best

Restaurant Price Code

Dollar signs reflect the average cost of a typical main course.

$$$$ **Splurge:** Most main courses over €15
$$$ **Pricier:** €10-15
$$ **Moderate:** €5-10
$ **Budget:** Under €5

Souvlaki and other takeaway food is **$**; a basic café or sit-down restaurant is **$$**; a casual but more upscale restaurant is **$$$**; and a swanky splurge is **$$$$**.

known are Savatiano (the most widely grown grape used for *retsina* and other wines), Assyrtiko (a crisp white mostly from Santorini), and Moschofilero (a dry white from the Peloponnese).

Other things to try are Greek **beer** (good local brands include Alpha, Fix, Vergina, and Mythos), or some special spirits. Cloudy, anise-flavored **ouzo** is worth a try even if you don't like the taste (black licorice). Ouzo turns from clear to milky white when you add ice or water (don't drink it straight). Greeks drink it both as an aperitif and with food. Even better is **tsipouro** (similar to Italian grappa), a brandy distilled from leftover grape skins and stems. **Metaxa** is to be savored after dinner. This rich, sweet, golden-colored liqueur has a brandy base blended with aged wine and a "secret" herbal mixture.

While most Greeks drink espresso, you can still seek out traditional **Greek coffee** (similar to Turkish coffee). In summer, cafés are filled with Greeks sipping **iced coffee** drinks. There are two types: *frappé* and *freddo*. Both are essentially cold coffee, whipped in a blender, and served over ice. *Frappé* is made with instant coffee (plus sometimes milk and sugar), while *freddo* is made with filtered coffee (from an espresso machine) and can be ordered as a *freddo espresso* (iced espresso, no milk) or *freddo cappuccino* (with cold foamed milk).

For something sweet, various bakeries around town sell takeaway portions of baklava, a classic Greek treat. Also try *bougatsa* (thin pastry with cream), *loukoumades* (fried Greek doughnuts), and *koulouri* (sesame bread rings).

Greek Cuisine

Greek food is simple...and simply delicious. Unlike the French or the Italians, who are forever experimenting to perfect an intricate cuisine, the Greeks found an easy formula and stick with it—and it rarely misses. The four Greek food groups are olives (and olive oil), salty feta cheese, ripe tomatoes, and crispy phyllo dough. Virtually every dish you'll have here is built on a foundation of these four tasty building blocks.

Although the Greeks don't like to admit it, their cuisine has a lot in common with Turkish food, including many of the same dishes. (This is partly because they share a similar climate, and partly because Greece was part of the Ottoman Empire for nearly 400 years.) Some names—such as moussaka—come directly from Turkish. You'll find traces of Italian influences as well, such as *pastitsio,* the "Greek lasagna."

My favorite fast, cheap, and filling Greek snack is souvlaki pita, a tasty shish kebab wrapped in flat bread. Souvlaki stands are all over Greece. Don't miss the creamy yogurt with honey. Feta cheese salads and flaky nut-and-honey baklava are two other tasty treats. Dunk your bread into *tzatziki* (TZAHT-zee-kee), the ubiquitous and refreshing cucumber-and-yogurt dip.

THE PLAKA

Avoid obvious, touristy joints on main pedestrian drag in favor of more authentic-feeling eateries huddled on quieter hillside just above, including the stepped lane called Mnisikleous (see map, page 182)

1   **$$ Geros tou Moria Tavern** Sprawling and venerable place, three eating areas: tour-group-friendly and air-conditioned indoor dining hall has live Greek music and dance, more intimate Palio Tetradio has a terrace, best of all are tables along the steps under grapevines (daily 9:00-24:00).
Mnisikleous 27, tel. 210-322-1753

2   **$$ Scholarhio Ouzeri Kouklis** Serves only small plates, jammed with tourists but fun and inexpensive, ideal for small groups wanting to try a variety of *mezedes,* choose from big platter of dishes, homemade booze, airy perch at top of the Plaka, 1930s atmosphere (daily 11:30-24:00).
Tripodon 14, tel. 210-324-7605

EATING

③ **$$$ Xenios Zeus (Ξένιος Ζευς)** Sits proudly at top of Mnisikleous steps, traditional, home-cooked Greek food, inside or outside seating on a terrace (daily 11:00-24:00, closed Nov-March).

Mnisikleous 37, tel. 210-324-9514

④ **$$ Klepsidra Café** On characteristic corner high in the Plaka, island ambience, tiny tables littering the ramshackle steps, somewhat younger and more local crowd, George and team serve light bites, good desserts, traditional coffee, and booze (daily 9:00-24:00).

Thrasivoulou 9, tel. 210-321-2493

⑤ **$$$ Palia Taverna tou Psara** Big, pricey eatery, open since 1898, live folk music generally Fri-Sat from 20:00, grand rooftop terrace (daily 12:00-24:00).

Eretheos 16, tel. 210-321-8734

NEAR SYNTAGMA SQUARE

Urban dining in a pleasantly less touristic area (see map, page 181)

⑥ **$$$$ 2Mazi Restaurant Wine Bar** Fills a tranquil and leafy courtyard, modern Greek gourmet cooking, stylish setting with equally stylish locals, reservations smart (daily 13:00-24:00).

Nikis 48, tel. 210-322-2839, www.2mazi.gr

⑦ **$$$ Tzitzikas Kai Mermigas** Serves modern regional Greek cuisine, two levels of indoor seating, fun and mod atmosphere, sidewalk tables (daily 12:30-24:00).

Mitropoleos 12, tel. 210-324-7607

⑧ **$$$ Avocado Vegetarian Café** Organic-food eatery serving pastas, pizzas, veggie burgers, sandwiches, and lots of energy juices (Mon-Sat 12:00-23:00, Sun until 19:00).

Nikis 30, tel. 210-323-7878

⑨ **$$ Kimolia (Κιμωλία) Art Café** Cute little place at edge of Plaka, light café fare at reasonable prices, relaxing vibe, friendly service (daily 10:00-24:00).

Iperidou 5, tel. 211-184-8446

⑩ **$$$ Athinaikon Restaurant** Venerable businessman's favorite, 1930s heritage, serves variety of traditional *mezedes*, no-nonsense art-deco/modern interior with professional service, local crowd, polished and international but affordable (Mon-Sat 12:00-24:00, Sun until 22:00).

Mitropoleos 34, tel. 210-325-2688

⑪ **$$$$ Black Duck Garden** Cozy urban oasis, tucked into courtyard of Museum of the City of Athens, fine place to slip away from the tourist crowds, short Mediterranean-focused menu, garden lit with candles and hanging lanterns at night (daily 10:00-24:00, closed in winter).

Ioannou Paparigopoulou 5, tel. 210-325-2396

⑫ **$$$$ Hotel Grande Bretagne's Roof Garden Restaurant** Posh as can be, pure fancy-hotel-restaurant elegance, rooftop garden with spectacular Acropolis views, reservations required for dinner (daily 13:00-24:00).

Syntagma Square, tel. 210-333-0766, www.gbroofgarden.gr

⑬ **$ Ariston (Αριστον)** In business for more than a century, one of Athens' top spots for savory pies, choose between *spanakopita* (spinach pie), *tiropita* (cheese pie), *kreatopita* (minced pork-meat pie), *meletzanitopita* (eggplant pie), and more, good desserts made with flaky phyllo (Mon, Wed, and Sat 7:30-18:00, Tue and Thu-Fri until 21:00, closed Sun).

Voulis 10, tel. 210-322-7626

IN AND NEAR PSYRRI

Fun area just north of Monastiraki with a unique charm (see map, page 182)

⑭ **$$ Taverna tou Psyrri (Η Ταβερνα του Ψυρρη)** In the heart of the restaurant action, garden terrace hidden in back, straightforward menu, good prices (daily 12:00-24:00).

Eschilou 12, tel. 210-321-4923

⑮ **$$ O Nikitas (Ο Νικήτας)** On a peaceful square, serves mainly *mezedes*, local crowd (Wed-Sat 12:00-23:00, Sun-Tue until 18:00).

Agion Anargyron 19, tel. 210-325-2591

⑯ **$$ Avli (Αυλή)** Thriving courtyard hidden behind speakeasy door and filled with a jumble of tiny tables, small and satisfying menu, specializes in a daily *mezedes* plate (daily 12:00-24:00).

Agiou Dimitriou 12—look for the small doorway labeled αυλή

⑰ **$$ Ta Karamanlidika tou Fani (Τα Καραμανλίδικα Του Φάνη)** Near Central Market, nice change of pace from typical Psyrri tavernas, quality meat-and-cheese shop that doubles as a restaurant, variety of tasty small plates, friendly service of Maria and her gang (Mon-Sat 12:00-23:00, closed Sun).

Evripidou 52, tel. 210-325-4184

⑱ **$$$ Melilotos (Μελίλωτοσ)** Near St. Irene Square, chic but accessible spot, indoor and outdoor seating on a lively lane, melds Greek ingredients and traditions with international influences (Mon-Wed 14:00-23:00, Thu-Sun from 12:00).

Kalamiotou 19, tel. 210-322-2458

⑲ **$ "Souvlaki Row"** Junction of Monastiraki Square and Mitropoleos street, trio of souvlaki restaurants—**Thanasis (Θανάσης)**, **Savvas (Σάββας)**, and **Bairaktaris (Μπαϊρακταρησ)**, souvlaki to go or dine-in service for more (all open daily until very late).

⑳ **$ Kosta (ΚΩΣΤΑ)** Hole-in-the-wall serving up good souvlaki pitas since the 1940s, no gyro slices or kebabs—just traditional €2 skewer-roasted souvlaki, get it to go or grab a stool on tiny square facing St. Irene's Church (Mon-Fri 9:00-18:00, closed Sat-Sun).

Off Aiolou Street two blocks north of Ermou

MAKRIGIANNI AND KOUKAKI

Area surrounding the Acropolis Museum is home to a trendy, touristy row of eateries along pedestrian Makrigianni street—and these recommended places (see map, page 182)

㉑ **$$$ Mani Mani (Μάνη Μάνη)** Cuisine and ingredients from the Mani Peninsula, food is thoughtfully updated Greek, dining indoors only, chef Alex cooks and wife Yolanda greets, reservations smart (daily 14:00-23:00 in summer, shorter hours off-season).

Upstairs at Falirou 10, tel. 210-921-8180, www.manimani.com.gr

㉒ **$$$$ Strofi Athenian Restaurant** White tablecloths, elegantly modern, rooftop Acropolis-view dining, attentive service, gorgeously presented plates, classic Greek cuisine, reservations smart—especially for rooftop seating (Tue-Sun 12:00-24:00, closed Mon).

Rovertou Galli 25, tel. 210-921-4130, www.strofi.gr

㉓ **$$$ Balcony** Upscale but unpretentious restaurant and bar, contemporary Greek cuisine accompanied by a good wine list, high-ceilinged dining room or roof garden with apartment-building views (daily 12:00-24:00).

Veikou 1, tel. 211-411-8437

㉔ **$$ To Kati Allo Restaurant (Το Κάτι Άλλο Ψησταριά)** Immediately under far side of Acropolis Museum, quintessential neighborhood hole-in-the-wall, run by English-speaking Kostas Bakatselos and his family, offers both sidewalk seating and fan-cooled inside tables, blackboard menu features short list of cheap and tasty local options (daily 11:00-24:00).

Chatzichristou 12, tel. 210-922-3071

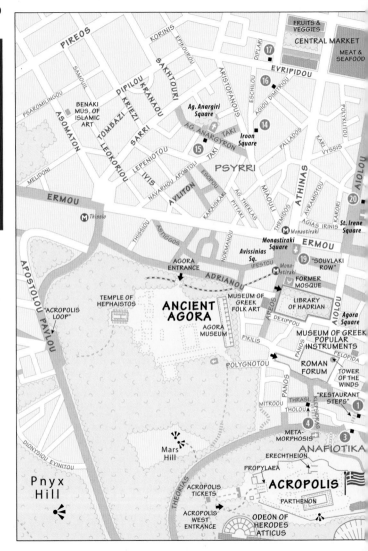

FRUITS & VEGGIES

CENTRAL MARKET

MEAT & SEAFOOD

PIREOS

KORINIS

EPHOUROU

SAMOUIL

DIPLARI

17

EVRIPIDOU

PSAROMILINGOU

ASOMATON

DIPILOU

KRIEZI

TOMBAZI

SAKHTOURI

KRANAOU

ARISTOFANOUS

AGIOU DIMITRIOU

ESCHILOU

16

BENAKI MUS. OF ISLAMIC ART

Ag. Anargiri Square

AG. ANARGYRON TAKI

POLYKLITOU

KARI

VYSSIS

SARRI

LEOKORIOU

Iroon Square

PALLADOS

14

MELIDONI

LEPENIOTOU

IVIS

15

TAKI

PSYRRI

AVLITON

NAVARHOU APOSTOLI

ESOPOLOU

AG. THEKLAS

MIAOULI

THEMIDOS

ATHINAS

AIOLOU

ERMOU

KARAISKAKI

PITTAKI

AVRAMIOTOU

AGIAS IRINIS

20

St. Irene Square

Thissio

THISSIOU

ASTIGGOS

NORMANOU

Monastiraki Square

Monastiraki

ERMOU

Avissinias Sq.

IFESTOU

Mona-stiraki

19

"SOUVLAKI ROW"

APOSTOLOU PAVLOU

AGORA ENTRANCE

ADRIANOU

FORMER MOSQUE

LIBRARY OF HADRIAN

AREOS

"ACROPOLIS LOOP"

TEMPLE OF HEPHAISTOS

ANCIENT AGORA

MUSEUM OF GREEK FOLK ART

DEXIPPOU

Agora Square

MUSEUM OF GREEK POPULAR INSTRUMENTS

AGORA MUSEUM

PIKILIS

PANOS

PELOPIDA

ROMAN FORUM

POLYGNOTOU

TOWER OF THE WINDS

MITROOU

PANOS

THRASL

LYSSIOU

LISIOU

"RESTAURANT STEPS"

1

THOLOU

4

3

Mars Hill

META-MORPHOSIS

ANAFIOTIKA

DIONYSIOU EYINITOU

ERECHTHEION

Pnyx Hill

THEORIAS

PROPYLAEA

ACROPOLIS

PARTHENON

ACROPOLIS TICKETS

ODEON OF HERODES ATTICUS

ACROPOLIS WEST ENTRANCE

Restaurants in Central Athens & Psyrri

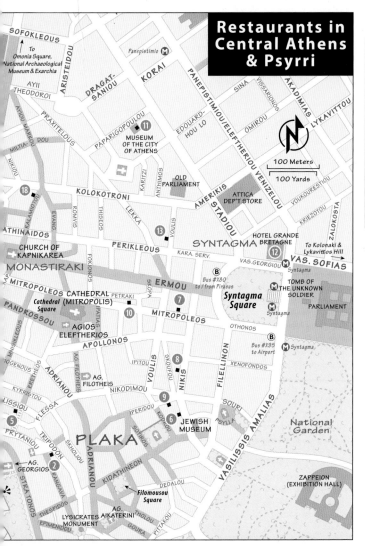

Makrigianni & Koukaki Restaurants

To Acropolis

To Plaka

DIONYSIOU AREOPAGITOU

150 Meters

150 Yards

ROVERTOU

KALLISPERI

MAKRIGIANNI

GARIVALDI

Filopappos
Hill

PROPYLEON

ERECHTHIOU

RATZIERI

GALLI

MITSEON

MAKRI

TZIREON

ACROPOLIS
MUSEUM

MAKRIGIANNI

PORINOU

Akropoli

SOFRONISKOU

PARTHENONOS

MISARALIOTOU

ZITROU

CHATZICHRISTOU

LEMBESI

24

STRATEON

FILOPAPPOS
MONUMENT

TZAMI

RENDI

KARATASI

23

MOUSON

LIAKOU

DRAKOU

GONI

VEIKOU

21

VOURVAHI

IOSIF TON ROGON

MARKOU BOTSARI

FALIROU

ANDREA SYNGROU

KORYZI

THEODOROU
NEGRI

FILOPAPPOU

TZAMI KARATASI

KARATZA

NOTI BOTSARI

ZAHARITSA

VEIKOU

NIKOLAOU DIMITRAKOPOULOU

PETMEZA

NAKOU

KALLIRROIS

SISMANI

ANASTASIOU

GOUFIE

ZINNI

ODYSSEOS

ANDROUTSOU

FALIROU

Syngrou-
Fix

ALIINOU

INGLESI

ALIINOU

THEOKRITOU

THEOKRITOU

IRAKLEOUS

KYNO-
SARGOUS

KOUKAKI

Practicalities

HELPFUL HINTS

Travel Tips

Travel Advisories: For updated health and safety conditions, including any restrictions for your destination, consult the US State Department's international travel website (www.travel.state.gov).

Tourist Information: The Greek National Tourist Organization (EOT), with its main branch near the Acropolis Museum, covers Athens and the rest of the country. Although their advice can be hit-or-miss, it's worth a stop to pick up their free city map, Athens Live booklet, and their slick, glossy book on Athens. They also have information on museums, entertainment options, bus and train connections, and a handy WC (Mon-Fri 8:00-21:00, Sat-Sun 10:00-18:00, shorter hours off-season; on pedestrian street leading to Acropolis Museum at Dionysiou Areopagitou 18, Metro: Akropoli; tel. 210-331-0392, www.visitgreece.gr, info@visitgreece.gr).

Time Zones: Greece is six/nine hours ahead of the East/West Coasts of the US. For a handy time converter, use the world clock app on your phone or download one (see www.timeanddate.com).

Hurdling the Language Barrier: Even though the Greek alphabet presents challenges to foreign visitors, communication is not hard. You'll find that most people in the tourist industry—and almost all young people—speak fine English. Many signs and menus (especially in Athens and major tourist spots) use both the Greek and our more familiar Latin alphabet. For Greek survival phrases, see the end of this chapter.

Business Hours: In Athens stores are generally open weekdays from 9:00 to 20:00 or later. Afternoon breaks are common, and Saturdays are like weekdays but with earlier closing hours.

Watt's Up: Europe's electrical system is 220 volts, instead of North America's 110 volts. Most electronics (laptops, phones, cameras) and appliances (newer hair dryers, CPAP machines) convert automatically, so you won't need a converter, but you will need an adapter plug with two round prongs, sold inexpensively at travel stores in the US.

Safety and Emergencies

Emergency and Medical Help: For any emergency service—ambulance, police, or fire—call **112** from a mobile phone or landline. If you get sick, do as the locals do and go to a pharmacist for advice. Or ask at

Helpful Websites

Greece's Tourist Information: www.visitgreece.gr
Athens Info: Greek Ministry of Culture (http://odysseus.culture.gr),
City of Athens Convention and Visitors Bureau (www.thisisathens.org),
Matt Barrett's Athens Survival Guide (www.athensguide.com)
Cheap Flights: Olympic (www.olympicair.com), Aegean (www.aegean
air.com), or try www.skyscanner.com
Athens Public Transit: www.oasa.gr
Greek Bus Help (unofficial): www.greeka.com/greece-travel/buses
Ferry Schedules for Greek Islands: www.gtp.gr, www.danae.gr/ferries-
Greece.asp, www.greekferries.gr

your hotel for help—they'll know the nearest medical and emergency services.

Theft or Loss: To replace a passport, you'll need to go in person to an embassy. If your credit and debit cards disappear, cancel and re-place them, and report the loss immediately (with a mobile phone, call these 24-hour US numbers: Visa—+1 303 967 1096, MasterCard—+1 636 722 7111, and American Express—+1 336 393 1111). For more information, see RickSteves.com/help.

Pickpocket Alert: Be wary of pickpockets, especially in crowds. Avoid carrying a wallet in your back pocket, and hold purses or small day bags in front, particularly at the following locations: Monastiraki flea market, Central Market, changing of the guard at the Tomb of the Unknown Soldier, major public transit routes (such as the Metro between the city and Piraeus or the airport), at the port, and on the main streets through the Plaka, such as Adrianou and Pandrossou.

Around Town

Traffic Alert: Streets that appear to be "traffic-free" often are shared by motorcycles, moped drivers, taxis, and delivery vans weaving their vehicles through the crowds. Keep your wits about you, and don't step into a street—even those that feel pedestrian-friendly—without looking both ways.

Slippery Streets: Athens has some marble-like streets and red pavement tiles that can be very slick, especially when it rains. Watch your step.

Laundry: A full-service launderette in the heart of the Plaka will wash, dry, and fold your clothes (same-day service if you drop off by noon; Mon and Wed 8:00-17:00, Tue and Thu-Fri until 20:00, closed Sat-Sun; Apollonos 17, tel. 210-323-2226). **Easywash** has self-service locations across the city (all open daily until midnight), including one in the Plaka (Adrianou 67, tel. 697-860-4401; http://easywashathens.gr).

ARRIVAL IN ATHENS

Eleftherios Venizelos International Airport

Athens' airport is at Spata, 17 miles east of downtown (code: ATH, www.aia.gr). This slick, user-friendly airport has two sections: B gates (serving European/Schengen countries—no passport control) and A gates (serving other destinations, including the US). Both sections feed into the same main terminal building (with a common baggage claim, ATMs, shops, car-rental counters, information desks, and additional services).

To get between the airport and downtown Athens, you have several options:

By Bus: Buses wait outside exit #5. Express bus #X95 costs €6 and operates 24 hours daily between the airport and Syntagma Square (3-5/hour, roughly 1 hour depending on traffic; tel. 11-185, www.oasa.gr). The downtown bus stop is on Othonos street, along the side of Syntagma Square.

By Metro: Line 3/blue zips you downtown in 45 minutes for €10 (2/hour, direction: Aghia Marina, daily 6:30-23:30; €18 for 2 people, €24 for 3, half-price for people under 18 or over 65, ticket good for 90 minutes on other Athens transit). Buy tickets at the machines or ticket window and follow signs down to the platforms. In downtown Athens, this train stops at Syntagma (where you can transfer to line 2/red) and Monastiraki (transfer to line 1/green).

To return to the airport by Metro, you can catch a train from Syntagma (2/hour, 5:30-24:00). Keep in mind that some Metro trains terminate at Doukissis Plakentias. If so, just hop off and wait—another train that continues to the airport should come along soon.

By Taxi or Uber: A well-marked taxi stand outside exit #3 offers fixed-price transfers that include all fees and tolls (€38 to central

Athens Transit

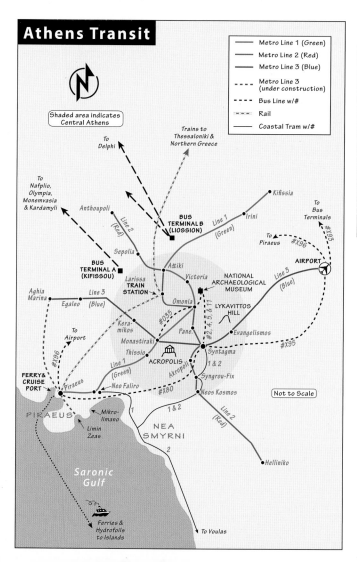

——	Metro Line 1 (Green)
——	Metro Line 2 (Red)
——	Metro Line 3 (Blue)
- - -	Metro Line 3 (under construction)
- - -	Bus Line w/#
×-×-×	Rail
——	Coastal Tram w/#

Shaded area indicates Central Athens

To Delphi

Trains to Thessaloniki & Northern Greece

To Nafplio, Olympia, Monemvasia & Kardamyli

Anthoupoli

Kifissia

Line 1 (Green)

Irini

To Bus Terminals #X95

Line 2 (Red)

BUS TERMINAL B (LIOSSION)

To Piraeus #X96

AIRPORT

Sepolia

Attiki

Victoria

Line 3 (Blue)

BUS TERMINAL A (KIFISSOU)

Larissa TRAIN STATION

NATIONAL ARCHAEOLOGICAL MUSEUM

Aghia Marina

Line 3 (Blue)

Egaleo

Omonia

#2, 4, 5, & 11

LYKAVITTOS HILL

To Airport

#196

Kerameikos

#055

Pane

Evangelismos

#X95

Monastiraki

Thissio

ACROPOLIS

Syntagma

1 & 2

FERRY & CRUISE PORT

Line 1 (Green)

Piraeus

Akropoli

Syngrou-Fix

Not to Scale

Neo Faliro

#X80

Neos Kosmos

PIRAEUS

Mikro-limano

1

1 & 2

Limin Zeas

NEA SMYRNI

Line 2 (Red)

Saronic Gulf

2

Helliniko

Ferries & Hydrofoils to Islands

To Voulas

Athens, covers up to 4 people, fare increases to €55 or more between 24:00 and 5:00). You can use Uber in Athens to get to and from the airport. In Athens, Uber operates as UberTaxi. You'll still book your ride through the app, but a taxi will pick you up. Rates to and from the airport are fixed, so Uber won't save you money on this route, but it's good for convenience and familiarity.

By Car Service: A variety of private services offer airport transfers for approximately the same cost as a taxi, but often with a nicer car and more personal and professional service. Consider **George's Taxi** (for 4 people or fewer, call Nikolas at 693-220-5887; for larger groups, call Billy at 697-443-0678; www.taxigreece.com, info@taxi greece.com); **Tune in Tours** (tel. 210-653-7209, mobile 697-320-1213, www.tuneintours.com); or **Athens Tour Taxi** (mobile 693-229-5395, www.athenstourtaxi.com, atsathens@gmail.com, Panagiotis and Konstantinos Tyrlis).

Athens' Port: Piraeus

Piraeus, a city six miles southwest of central Athens, is the main port for services to the Greek islands. While the port is vast, most of it is used for ferry traffic; all cruise ships moor at one end.

To get from the Piraeus ferry terminals to Athens, you have a few options:

By Train: Metro line 1/green conveniently links Piraeus with downtown Athens (€1.40, good for 90 minutes including transfers, departs about every 10-15 minutes between 6:00 and 24:00). The Metro station is in a big, yellow Neoclassical building near gate E6. Buy your ticket from a machine, validate it, and hop on the train.

By Taxi: A taxi between Piraeus and downtown Athens should cost about €25, and can take anywhere from 20-40 minutes, depending on traffic and on your starting/ending point at Piraeus. Uber works well and is often cheaper.

From Piraeus Cruise Terminals to Athens: Cruise-ship passengers unload at the far-south end of the port. Because the Metro station is a 20-40-minute walk from here, take a taxi or Uber, hire a private driver, or ask at the terminal about public bus #X80 or one of the hop-on, hop-off buses that goes to Athens (www.citysightseeing.gr or www.athensopentour.com).

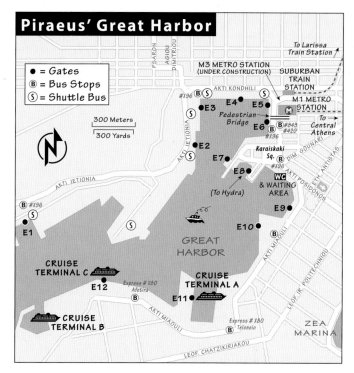

Piraeus' Great Harbor

- ● = Gates
- Ⓑ = Bus Stops
- Ⓢ = Shuttle Bus

300 Meters
300 Yards

To Larissa Train Station

M3 METRO STATION (UNDER CONSTRUCTION)

SUBURBAN TRAIN STATION

M1 METRO STATION

To Central Athens

PSARON

AGIOU DIMITRIOU

AKTI KONDHILI

#196 Ⓑ Ⓢ

Ⓢ E4 E5

● E3

Pedestrian Bridge

E6 ●

Ⓑ #843 #420

AKTI IETIONIA

#196

● E2

Ⓢ

Karaiskaki Sq.

E7 ●

Ⓑ #196

E8 ●

WC & WAITING AREA

AKTI POSIDONOS

ELETH ANTISTAS

DIM. GOUNARI

(To Hydra)

E9 ●

Ⓑ #196

Ⓢ

E1

Ⓢ

E10 ●

Ⓑ

AKTI MIAOULI

GREAT HARBOR

CRUISE TERMINAL C

E12

Express # X80 Afetiria

Ⓑ

CRUISE TERMINAL A

E11 ●

LEOF. IR. POLITECHNIOU

CRUISE TERMINAL B

AKTI MIAOULI

Express # X80 Teloneio

Ⓑ

ZEA MARINA

LEOF. CHATZIKIRIAKOU

AKTI IETIONIA

GETTING AROUND ATHENS

The tourist core of Athens is surprisingly walkable. Many travelers find they don't need to take any public transit at all, once they're settled into their hotel. But for a longer visit, it's smart to get comfortable with public transportation, which is useful for reaching the National Archaeological Museum, the port of Piraeus, and the airport.

By Public Transportation

Athens' buses, trams, and Metro use the same ticketing system. Note that the city is gradually transitioning from single-use paper tickets to multiride "passes" and a smart card system that's reusable and re-chargeable. Be prepared for either system to be in place.

A **basic ticket** (€1.40, or just €0.60 if over 65 or under 18) is good for 90 minutes on all public transit and covers transfers. The **multi-ride** passes are available as paper tickets with 2, 5, or 11 rides (appears as "10+1" on ticket machines). They offer a slight per-ride discount, and do not expire—but cannot be shared between people.

If planning more than three rides in a day, consider the **24-hour ticket** (€4.50); for a longer visit using lots of public transit, you might get your money's worth with a **five-day ticket** (€9).

If starting and finishing at the airport, consider the **three-day tourist ticket** (€22), which includes a round-trip airport transfer on the Metro or Express bus #X95 as well as unlimited in-city travel on all Metro lines, the suburban railway (*Proastiakos*), the tram, and bus.

When using the Metro, you'll need to scan your ticket at the turn-stile each time you start and end a journey. For buses, scan your ticket as you board. Those riding without a ticket (or with an unscanned ticket) are subject to stiff fines.

Metro: The Metro is the most straightforward way to get around Athens—it's slick and user-friendly. Just look for signs with a blue *M* in a green circle. Signs are in both Greek and English, as are announcements inside subway cars, and electronic reader boards on the platforms show which exits have escalators going up or down. Trains run every few minutes on weekdays and slightly less frequently on weekends (5:30-24:00, later on Fri-Sat, www.stasy.gr).

The Metro lines are color-coded and numbered. Use the end-of-the-line stops to figure out which direction you need to go.

Line 1 (green) runs from the port of Piraeus in the southwest to Kifissia in the northern suburbs. Key stops include: **Piraeus** (boats to the islands), **Thissio** (enjoyable neighborhood with good restaurants and nightlife), **Monastiraki** (city center), **Omonia** (15-minute walk from National Archaeological Museum), and **Victoria** (10-minute walk from National Archaeological Museum). Transfer to line 2 at Omonia and to line 3 at Monastiraki (sometimes labeled "Monastirion").

Line 2 (red) runs from Anthoupoli in the northwest to Helliniko (Elliniko) in the southeast. Important stops include: **Larissa Station** (train station), **Omonia** (National Archaeological Museum), **Syntagma**

(city center), **Akropoli** (Acropolis and Makrigianni/Koukaki hotel neighborhood), and **Syngrou-Fix** (Makrigianni/Koukaki hotels). Transfer to line 1 at Omonia and to line 3 at Syntagma.

Line 3 (blue) runs from Aghia Marina in the west to the airport in the east. Important stops are: **Keramikos** (near Keramikos Cemetery and the lively Gazi district), **Monastiraki** (city center), **Syntagma** (city center), **Evangelismos** (Kolonaki neighborhood, with good museums), and **Airport** (requires a separate ticket). Transfer to line 1 at Monastiraki and to line 2 at Syntagma. Line 3 is being extended past Aghia Marina, into Piraeus (the new Piraeus station will open right next to the original one).

Bus: In general, I'd avoid Athens' slow and overcrowded buses (taxis and UberTaxi are cheap and easy), but there are a few exceptions: Buses **#2, #4, #5,** and **#11** run from Syntagma north up the busy Eleftheriou Venizelou corridor, bearing right on 28 Oktovriou and stopping near the National Archaeological Museum (at the Polytechneio stop). From near Monastiraki (on Athinas street), bus **#035** also gets you to the National Archaeological Museum.

By Taxi

Athens is a great taxi town. Its yellow taxis are cheap and handy (€3.50 minimum charge covers most short rides in town; after that it's €0.74/km—tariff 1 on the meter). To avoid rip-offs, make sure the meter is on and set to tariff 1 (unless it's the middle of the night when it's tariff 2). Find out in advance roughly how much the fare should be (ask at hotel or restaurant). If traveling out of the city, it's better to negotiate a rate up front rather than use the meter.

Uber operates as UberTaxi in Athens. (You book your ride through the app, but a taxi picks you up.) Uber is generally cheaper than hailing a cab (often even half the cost, except for rides to and from the airport where there's no savings). Note there is a €3 minimum charge.

MONEY

Greece uses the Euro currency: 1 euro (€) = about $1.20. To convert prices in euros to dollars, add about 20 percent: €20 = about $24, €50 = about $60. (Check www.oanda.com for the latest exchange rates.)

Tipping

Tipping in Greece isn't as automatic and generous as it is in the US, but some general guidelines apply.

Restaurants: At Greek restaurants that have waitstaff, locals generally round up their bill after a good meal (usually about 10 percent).

Taxis: For a typical ride, round up your fare a bit (for instance, if the fare is €4.50, pay €5).

Services: In general, if someone in the service industry does a super job for you, a small tip of a euro or two is appropriate...but not required. If you're not sure whether (or how much) to tip for a service, ask a local for advice.

Here's my basic strategy for using money in Greece:

Upon arrival, head for an ATM at the airport and withdraw some local currency, using a debit card with low international transaction fees.

In general, pay for bigger expenses with a credit card and use cash for smaller purchases. Use a debit card only for cash withdrawals. Although credit cards are widely accepted in Europe, cash is sometimes the only way to pay for cheap food, bus fare, taxis, tips, and local guides. Some businesses (especially smaller ones, such as B&Bs and mom-and-pop cafés and shops) may charge you extra for using a credit card—or might not accept credit cards at all. Having cash on hand helps you out of a jam if your card randomly doesn't work. Keep your cards and cash safe in a money belt.

US credit cards generally work fine in Europe—with a few exceptions. European cards use chip-and-PIN technology; most chip cards issued in the US instead require a signature. When presented with a US card, European card readers may generate a receipt for you to sign—or prompt you to enter your PIN.

At self-service payment machines (such as transit-ticket kiosks), US cards may not work. In this case, look for a cashier who can process your card manually—or pay in cash.

Making International Calls

For the dialing instructions below, use the complete phone number, including the area code (if there is one), but drop the initial zero except when calling Italy.

From a Mobile Phone: It's easy to dial with a mobile phone. Whether calling from the US to Europe, country to country within Europe, or from Europe to the US—it's all the same: Press zero until you get a + sign, enter the country code (30 for Greece), then dial the phone number.

From a US Landline to Europe: Dial 011 (US/Canada access code), country code (30 for Greece), and phone number.

From a European Landline to the US or Europe: Dial 00 (Europe access code), country code (1 for the US), and phone number. For more phoning help, see www.howtocallabroad.com.

Using Your Phone in Europe

Sign up for an international plan. To stay connected at a lower cost, sign up for an international service plan through your carrier. Most providers offer a simple bundle that includes calling, messaging, and data.

Use free Wi-Fi whenever possible. Unless you have an unlimited-data plan, save most of your online tasks for Wi-Fi. Most accommodations in Europe offer free Wi-Fi, and many cafés offer hotspots for customers. You may also often find Wi-Fi at TIs, city squares, major museums, public-transit hubs, airports, and aboard trains and buses.

Minimize the use of your cellular network. Even with an international-data plan, wait until you're on Wi-Fi to Skype, download apps, stream videos, or do other megabyte-greedy tasks. Using a navigation app such as Google Maps over a cellular network can require lots of data, so download maps when you're on Wi-Fi, then use the app offline.

Use Wi-Fi calling and messaging apps. Skype, WhatsApp, FaceTime, and Google Hangouts are great for making free or low-cost calls or sending texts over Wi-Fi worldwide.

RESOURCES FROM RICK STEVES

Begin Your Trip at RickSteves.com: This guidebook is just one of many titles in my series on European travel. I also produce a public television series, Rick Steves' Europe, and a public radio show, Travel with Rick Steves. My mobile-friendly website is the place to explore Europe in preparation for your trip. You'll find thousands of fun articles, videos, and radio interviews; a wealth of money-saving tips; travel news dispatches; a video library of travel talks; my travel blog; our latest guidebook updates (RickSteves.com/update); and the free Rick Steves Audio Europe app. You can also follow me on Facebook, Instagram, and Twitter.

Packing Checklist

Clothing

- ☐ 5 shirts: long- & short-sleeve
- ☐ 2 pairs pants (or skirts/capris)
- ☐ 1 pair shorts
- ☐ 5 pairs underwear & socks
- ☐ 1 pair walking shoes
- ☐ Sweater or warm layer
- ☐ Rainproof jacket with hood
- ☐ Tie, scarf, belt, and/or hat
- ☐ Swimsuit
- ☐ Sleepwear/loungewear

Money

- ☐ Debit card(s)
- ☐ Credit card(s)
- ☐ Hard cash (US $100-200)
- ☐ Money belt

Documents

- ☐ Passport
- ☐ Tickets & confirmations: flights, hotels, trains, rail pass, car rental, sight entries
- ☐ Driver's license
- ☐ Student ID, hostel card, etc.
- ☐ Photocopies of important documents
- ☐ Insurance details
- ☐ Guidebooks & maps
- ☐ Notepad & pen
- ☐ Journal

Toiletries Kit

- ☐ Soap, shampoo, toothbrush, toothpaste, floss, deodorant, sunscreen, brush/comb, etc.
- ☐ Medicines & vitamins
- ☐ First-aid kit
- ☐ Glasses/contacts/sunglasses
- ☐ Sewing kit
- ☐ Packet of tissues (for WC)
- ☐ Earplugs

Electronics

- ☐ Mobile phone
- ☐ Camera & related gear
- ☐ Tablet/ebook reader/laptop
- ☐ Headphones/earbuds
- ☐ Chargers & batteries
- ☐ Plug adapters

Miscellaneous

- ☐ Daypack
- ☐ Sealable plastic baggies
- ☐ Laundry supplies
- ☐ Small umbrella
- ☐ Travel alarm/watch

Optional Extras

- ☐ Second pair of shoes
- ☐ Travel hairdryer
- ☐ Water bottle
- ☐ Fold-up tote bag
- ☐ Small flashlight & binoculars
- ☐ Small towel or washcloth
- ☐ Tiny lock
- ☐ Extra passport photos

Greek Survival Phrases

Knowing a few phrases of Greek can help if you're traveling off the beaten path. Just learning the pleasantries (such as please and thank you) will improve your connections with locals, even in the bigger cities.

Because Greek words can be transliterated differently in English, I've also included the Greek spellings. Note that in Greek, a semicolon is used the same way we use a question mark.

Hello. (formal)	Gia sas. Γειά σας.	yah sahs
Hi. / Bye. (informal)	Gia. Γειά.	yah
Do you speak English?	Milate anglika? Μιλάτε αγγλικά; mee-**lah**-teh ahn-glee-**kah**	
Yes. / No.	Ne. / Ohi. Ναι. / Όχι.	neh / **oh**-hee
I (don't) understand.	(Den) katalaveno. (Δεν) καταλαβαίνω. (dehn) kah-tah-lah-**veh**-noh	
Please. (Also: You're welcome).	Parakalo. Παρακαλώ.	pah-rah-kah-**loh**
Thank you (very much)	Efharisto (poli). Ευχαριστώ (πολύ). ehf-hah-ree-**stoh** (poh-**lee**)	
Excuse me.	Sygnomi. Συγνώμη.	seeg-**noh**-mee
Goodbye.	Antio. Αντίο.	ahd-**yoh** (think "adieu")
one / two / three	ena / dio / tria ένα / δύο / τρία **eh**-nah / **dee**-oh / **tree**-ah	
How much?	Poso kani? Πόσο κάνει;	**poh**-soh **kah**-nee
I'd like / We'd like...	Tha ithela / Tha thelame... Θα ήθελα / Θα θέλαμε... thah **ee**-theh-lah / thah **theh**-lah-meh	
...a room.	...ena dhomatio. ...ένα δωμάτιο. **eh**-nah doh-**mah**-tee-oh	
...a ticket.	...ena isitirio. ...ένα εισιτήριο. **eh**-nah ee-see-**tee**-ree-oh	
Where is...?	Pou ine...? Που είναι...;	poo **ee**-neh
...the station	...o stathmos ...ο σταθμός	oh **stahth**-mohs
...the tourist office	...to grafeio touriston ...το γραφείο τουριστών too grah-**fee**-oh too-ree-**stohn**	
toilet	toualeta τουαλέτα	twah-**leh**-tah
men / women	andres / gynekes άντρες / γυναικες **ahn**-drehs / yee-**neh**-kehs	
left / right / straight	dexia / aristera / efthia δεξιά / αριστερά / ευθεία dehk-see-**ah** / ah-ree-steh-**rah** / ehf-**thee**-ah	

In a Restaurant

I'd like to reserve...	Tha ithela na kliso... Θα ήθελα να κλείσω... thah **ee**-theh-lah nah **klee**-soh
...a table for one / two.	...ena trapezi gia enan / dio. ...ένα τραπέζι για έναν / δύο. **eh**-nah trah-**peh**-zee yah **eh**-nahn / **dee**-oh
The menu (in English).	Ton katalogo (sta anglika). Τον κατάλογο (στα αγγλικά). tohn kah-**tah**-loh-goh (stah ahn-glee-**kah**)
service (not) included	to servis (den) perilamvanete το σέρβις (δεν) περιλαμβάνεται toh **sehr**-vees (dehn) peh-ree-lahm-**vah**-neh-teh
"to go"	gia exo για έξω yah **ehk**-soh
with / without	me / horis με / χωρίς meh / hoh-**rees**
and / or	ke / i και / ή keh / ee
appetizers	proto piato πρώτο πιάτο **proh**-toh pee-**ah**-toh
bread / cheese	psomi / tiri ψωμί / τυρί psoh-**mee** / tee-**ree**
sandwich	sandwich σάντουιτς "sandwich"
soup / salad	soupa / salata σούπα / σαλάτα **soo**-pah / sah-**lah**-tah
meat / poultry / fish	kreas / poulerika / psari κρέας / πουλερικα / ψάρι **kray**-ahs / poo-leh-ree-**kah** / **psah**-ree
fruit / vegetables	frouta / lahanika φρούτα / λαχανικά **froo**-tah / lah-hah-nee-**kah**
dessert	gliko γλυκό lee-**koh**
coffee / tea / water	kafes / tsai / nero καφές / τσάι / νερο kah-**fehs** / **chah**-ee / neh-**roh**
wine / beer	krasi / bira κρασί / μπύρα krah-**see** / **bee**-rah
red / white	kokkino / aspro κόκκινο / άσπρο **koh**-kee-noh / **ah**-sproh
glass / bottle	potiri / boukali ποτήρι / μπουκάλι poh-**tee**-ree / boo-**kah**-lee
(To your) health! (like "Cheers!")	(Stin i) gia mas! (Στην υ) γειά μας! (stee nee) yah mahs
Enjoy your meal.	Kali orexi !Καλή όρεξη! kah-**lee** oh-**rehk**-see
Bill, please.	Ton logariasmo parakalo. Τον λογαριασμό παρακαλώ. tohn loh-gah-ree-ahs-**moh** pah-rah-kah-**loh**

INDEX

Start your trip at

Our website enhances this book and turns

Explore Europe

At ricksteves.com you can browse through thousands of articles, videos, photos and radio interviews, plus find a wealth of money-saving travel tips for planning your dream trip. And with our mobile-friendly website, you can easily access all this great travel information anywhere you go.

TV Shows

Preview the places you'll visit by watching entire half-hour episodes of *Rick Steves' Europe* (choose from all 100 shows) on-demand, for free.

ricksteves.com

your travel dreams into affordable reality

Radio Interviews

Enjoy ready access to Rick's vast library of radio interviews covering travel tips and cultural insights that relate specifically to your Europe travel plans.

Travel Forums

Learn, ask, share! Our online community of savvy travelers is a great resource for first-time travelers to Europe, as well as seasoned pros.

Travel News

Subscribe to our free Travel News e-newsletter, and get monthly updates from Rick on what's happening in Europe.

Classroom Europe

Check out our free resource for educators with 400+ short video clips from the *Rick Steves' Europe* TV show.

Audio Europe™

Rick's Free Travel App

Get your FREE Rick Steves Audio Europe™ app to enjoy…

- Dozens of self-guided tours of Europe's top museums, sights and historic walks
- Hundreds of tracks filled with cultural insights and sightseeing tips from Rick's radio interviews
- All organized into handy geographic playlists
- For Apple and Android

With Rick whispering in your ear, Europe gets even better.

Find out more at ricksteves.com

Pack Light and Right

Gear up for your next adventure at ricksteves.com

Light Luggage

Pack light and right with Rick Steves' affordable, custom-designed rolling carry-on bags, backpacks, day packs and shoulder bags.

Accessories

From packing cubes to moneybelts and beyond, Rick has personally selected the travel goodies that will help your trip go smoother.

Shop at ricksteves.com

Rick Steves has

Save time and energy

This guidebook is your independent-travel toolkit. But for all it delivers, it's still up to you to devote the time and energy it takes to manage the preparation and logistics that are essential for a happy trip. If that's a hassle, there's a solution.

Rick Steves Tours

A Rick Steves tour takes you to Europe's most interesting places with great guides and small groups.

great tours, too!

with minimum stress

We follow Rick's favorite itineraries, ride in comfy buses, stay in family-run hotels, and bring you intimately close to the Europe you've traveled so far to see. Most importantly, we take away the logistical headaches so you can focus on the fun.

Join the fun

This year we'll take thousands of free-spirited travelers—nearly half of them repeat customers—along with us on four dozen different itineraries, from Ireland to Italy to Athens. Is a Rick Steves tour the right fit for your travel dreams? Find out at ricksteves.com, where you can check seat availability and sign up.

Europe is best experienced with happy travel partners. We hope you can join us.

See our itineraries at ricksteves.com

A Guide for Every Trip

BEST OF GUIDES

Full-color guides in an easy-to-scan format, focusing on top sights and experiences in popular destinations

Best of England
Best of Europe
Best of France
Best of Germany

Best of Ireland
Best of Italy
Best of Scotland
Best of Spain

COMPREHENSIVE GUIDES

City, country, and regional guides printed on Bible-thin paper. Packed with detailed coverage for a multi-week trip exploring iconic sights and more

Amsterdam &
  the Netherlands
Barcelona
Belgium: Bruges, Brussels,
  Antwerp & Ghent
Berlin
Budapest
Croatia & Slovenia
Eastern Europe
England
Florence & Tuscany
France
Germany
Great Britain
Greece: Athens &
  the Peloponnese
Iceland

Ireland
Istanbul
Italy
London
Paris
Portugal
Prague & the Czech Republic
Provence & the French
  Riviera
Rome
Scandinavia
Scotland
Sicily
Spain
Switzerland
Venice
Vienna, Salzburg & Tirol

Many guides are available as ebooks.

POCKET GUIDES
Compact guides for shorter city trips

Amsterdam	Italy's Cinque Terre	Prague
Athens	London	Rome
Barcelona	Munich & Salzburg	Venice
Florence	Paris	Vienna

SNAPSHOT GUIDES
Focused single-destination coverage

Basque Country: Spain & France
Copenhagen & the Best of Denmark
Dublin
Dubrovnik
Edinburgh
Hill Towns of Central Italy
Krakow, Warsaw & Gdansk
Lisbon
Loire Valley
Madrid & Toledo
Milan & the Italian Lakes District
Naples & the Amalfi Coast
Nice & the French Riviera
Normandy
Northern Ireland
Norway
Reykjavík
Rothenburg & the Rhine
Sevilla, Granada & Southern Spain
St. Petersburg, Helsinki & Tallinn
Stockholm

CRUISE PORTS GUIDES
Reference for cruise ports of call

Mediterranean Cruise Ports
Scandinavian & Northern European
   Cruise Ports

TRAVEL SKILLS & CULTURE
Greater information and insight

Europe 101
Europe Through the Back Door
Europe's Top 100 Masterpieces
European Christmas
European Easter
European Festivals
For the Love of Europe
Travel as a Political Act

PHRASE BOOKS & DICTIONARIES

French
French, Italian & German
German
Italian
Portuguese
Spanish

PLANNING MAPS

Britain, Ireland & London
Europe
France & Paris
Germany, Austria & Switzerland
Iceland
Ireland
Italy
Scotland
Spain & Portugal

PHOTO CREDITS

Avalon Travel
Hachette Book Group
1700 Fourth Street
Berkeley, CA 94710

Printed in China by RR Donnelley
Third Edition
First printing January 2021

ISBN 978-1-64171-319-1

For the latest on Rick's talks, guidebooks, tours, public television series, and public radio show, contact Rick Steves' Europe, 130 Fourth Avenue North, Edmonds, WA 98020, 425/771-8303, RickSteves.com, rick@ricksteves.com.

Rick Steves' Europe
Managing Editor: Jennifer Madison Davis
Assistant Managing Editor: Cathy Lu
Editors: Glenn Eriksen, Suzanne Kotz, Rosie Leutzinger, Teresa Nemeth, Jessica Shaw, Carrie Shepherd, Meg Sneeringer
Editorial & Production Assistant: Megan Simms
Researcher: Robyn Stencil
Graphic Content Director: Sandra Hundacker
Maps & Graphics: David C. Hoerlein, Lauren Mills, Mary Rostad
Digital Asset Coordinator: Orin Dubrow

Avalon Travel
Senior Editor and Series Manager: Madhu Prasher
Associate Managing Editors: Jamie Andrade, Sierra Machado
Indexer: Claire Splan
Production & Typesetting: Rue Flaherty
Cover Design: Kimberly Glyder Design
Interior Design: Darren Alessi
Maps & Graphics: Kat Bennett, Mike Morgenfeld

Although every effort was made to ensure that the information was correct at the time of going to press, the author and publisher do not assume and hereby disclaim any liability to any party for any loss or damage caused by errors, omissions, bad souvlaki, or any potential travel disruption due to labor or financial difficulty, whether such errors or omissions result from negligence, accident, or any other cause.

Let's Keep on Travelin'

Your trip doesn't need to end.

Follow Rick on social media!

NOV 24 2021